Civil Procedure in Spain

Civil Procedure in Spain

Second Edition

Fernando Castillo Rigabert

This book was originally published as a monograph in the International Encyclopaedia of Laws/Civil Procedure.

Founding Editor: Roger Blanpain
General Editor: Frank Hendrickx
Volume Editor: Piet Taelman

Wolters Kluwer

Published by:
Kluwer Law International B.V.
PO Box 316
2400 AH Alphen aan den Rijn
The Netherlands
E-mail: international-sales@wolterskluwer.com
Website: lrus.wolterskluwer.com

Sold and distributed in North, Central and South America by:
Wolters Kluwer Legal & Regulatory U.S.
7201 McKinney Circle
Frederick, MD 21704
United States of America
Email: customer.service@wolterskluwer.com

Sold and distributed in all other countries by:
Air Business Subscriptions
Rockwood House
Haywards Heath
West Sussex
RH16 3DH
United Kingdom
Email: international-customerservice@wolterskluwer.com

Printed on acid-free paper

ISBN 978-94-035-0694-4

e-Book: ISBN 978-94-035-0695-1
web-PDF: ISBN 978-94-035-0700-2

Printed in the United Kingdom.

The Author

Fernando Castillo Rigabert has a doctorate in Law. He is Professor of Civil and Criminal Procedure in the Law School of the University of Murcia, Spain, and has taught Constitutional Procedure in the School of Law Practice of the same university. He has held the positions of 'Secretario General' of the University and Secretary of the School of Law Practice.

He has served as a judge in the Superior Court of Justice of the Autonomous Region of Murcia within the Administrative Chamber.

In recognition for his long-standing work training new lawyers, he was distinguished as an honorary member of the Bar Association in Murcia.

He has written several books and articles on civil, criminal, labour and constitutional procedure.

The Author

Table of Contents

List of Abbreviations

CC	Código Civil (Civil Code)
CE	Constitución Española (Spanish Constitution)
CP	Código Penal (Penal Code)
EGA	Estatuto General de la Abogacía (General Statute of Lawyers)
LA	Ley de Arbitraje (Arbitration Law)
LAJG	Ley de Asistencia Jurídica Gratuita (Law of Free Legal Aid)
LCJI	Ley de Cooperación Jurídica Internacional (International Cooperation in Civil and Commercial Matters Law)
LEC	Ley de Enjuiciamiento Civil de 1881 (Old Code of Civil Procedure)
LJV	Ley de Jurisdicción Voluntaria (Voluntary Jurisdiction Law)
LOCGPJ	Ley Orgánica del Consejo General del Poder Judicial (Organic Law of the General Council of the Judiciary)
LOPJ	Ley Orgánica del Poder Judicial (Organic Law of the Judicial Power)
LOTJ	Ley Orgánica del Tribunal del Jurado (Organic Law of Jury Trial)
NCCP	Ley de Enjuiciamiento Civil 1/2000, (New Code of Civil Procedure)
RD	Royal Decree
TC	Tribunal Constitucional (Constitutional Court)
TS	Tribunal Supremo (Supreme Court)

List of Abbreviations

General Introduction

§1. General Background

1. After the long period of General Franco's dictatorship (1939–1975), a new Constitution was approved in 1978 and Spain became a parliamentary monarchy. According to Article 1 of the Constitution, Spain is a 'social and democratic state' and 'liberty, justice, equality and politic pluralism are superior values of the legal system'. Article 2 states that the Constitution lies on the indissoluble unity of the Spanish nation, but it recognizes and guarantees autonomy for nationalities and regions. In other words, Spain is not a unitary State. It is divided into seventeen 'autonomous communities' plus two 'autonomous cities' (Ceuta and Melilla in northern Africa). Each community has a large level of autonomy with elected parliament and Government, but there is only one judicial system for the whole country.

2. The national Parliament ('Las Cortes Generales') is bicameral. It is elected for a four-year term, but early elections are possible in certain cases. The lower camera is called 'Congreso de los Diputados' and the upper camera is the Senate ('El Senado'). Congress elects the Prime Minister and he chooses the members of the cabinet.

3. Spain is not a confessional State, it is a civil State, but Article 16 of the Constitution reads that the State has to consider the religious beliefs of the Spanish people and has to cooperate with the Catholic Church and other religious denominations.

§2. Delimitation of the Subject Matter and Distinction with Other Types of Procedure

4. The Spanish Court system consists of different types of jurisdictions:

(a) The Constitutional Court (Tribunal Constitucional (TC)) deals with three main matters:
   - it controls the conformity of the acts passed by Parliament with the Constitution;
   - it protects fundamental rights at the highest level; and

– it decides the possible conflicts of competence between central State and autonomous regions.

(b) Ordinary jurisdiction is divided as follows:
   (i) civil – includes civil and commercial cases and it solves private conflicts between private people;
   (ii) criminal – criminal courts deal with the possible punishment of crimes and misdemeanours;
   (iii) administrative – administrative courts control the activity of Public Administration and the Government; and finally,
   (iv) social courts that deal with labour and social security cases. Every one of them has its own rules of procedure. The present monograph refers only to civil procedure as stated in b (i) above.

There are also military courts with its own rules.

§3. Sources of Civil Procedure Law

5. The Constitution is the first source of procedural law. It has several rules of this type: Articles 117–127 (ruling the 'Judicial Power'), Articles 159–165 (TC), Articles 15, 17, 18, 22, 24, 25. Among the fundamental rights, there are several that refer to the judiciary and the rights of the people before the courts for example Articles 53, 106. In several cases, ordinary judges must directly apply most of these norms, *per exemplum*, the rules that refer to civil liberties and fundamental rights.

6. The present code of civil procedure ('Ley de Enjuiciamiento Civil', Ley 1/2000) is in force since 8 January 2001. It substitutes the old code that was published in 1881. The code is divided into a preliminary title and four books. Each book is divided into titles, each title into chapters, the chapters into sections and each section into articles. The code has 827 articles. It is considerably shorter than the old one that had 2182, but we have to keep in mind that the actual code does not include bankruptcy or voluntary jurisdiction. The law is new, but is influenced by the old one. Technically, it is better and has resolved a lot of problems that the jurisprudence showed in the last century.

New Code of Civil Procedure (Ley de Enjuiciamiento Civil 1/2000 (NCCP)) has been amended by Law 13/2009 of November 3, to implement the so-called Judicial Office. Under the new law, the ' Secretario Judicial' (Deputy Clerk) has greater powers and solves a number of procedural issues.

The legislative activity affecting the civil process has been quite intense in recent years. Among others, Law 17/2011 of October 10 has been approved which amended several articles of the NCCP to achieve simpler procedures, especially in the area of appeals; Law 1/2013 of May 7 has as its main purpose to increase the guarantees of mortgagors; Law 19/2015 of July 13 amends articles concerning judicial auctions and, finally, Law 42/2015 of October 5, the purpose of which is to adjust the civil process to new communication technologies.

§4. General Features of the Administration of Justice in Civil Matters

I. Characteristics of the Procedure

7. Civil procedure, except in special matters, is based on an adversary system. The parties have to present the case before the judge. The parties, or their representatives ('procuradores' y 'abogados'), bring forward to the judge the facts, evidence and the qualification in law on which the judge bases his decision. Nevertheless, the system has always recognized the power of the judges regarding procedural matters and the subsequent possibility of 'ex officio' control of jurisdiction, competence and other subjects like due representation or capacity of the parties. But in essence, the adversary principle governs the procedure.

There are different types of procedure in Spanish law, but basically the proceedings are as follows: The trial begins with written pleadings, the evidence is usually oral and it is held in a hearing and the final statements are also oral.

II. Fundamental Guarantees

8. Article 24.1 of the Constitution states that everyone has the right to be protected by judges in their rights and legitimate interests. In other words, this fundamental right means that the judges have to respond to all the cases brought before them, when all the procedural requisites are fulfilled. The judge has to give a judgment according to law and has to motivate it, according to Article 120.2 of the Constitution. That means that the law imposes the requirement that the reason upon which a judgment is based should be made explicit.

9. The principle of the publicity of the hearing is set in Article 120.1 of the Constitution and also in Article 232 LOPJ and Article 138 NCCP. Nevertheless, there are a few exceptions, especially in family cases (divorce, etc.).

10. According to the Constitution the judiciary is the third power of the State and is governed by the General Council of the Judiciary (Consejo General del Poder Judicial). Judges and the courts exercise this 'power'. The Constitution states that judges and magistrates are independent, with security of tenure but subject to removal for cause and also that they are responsible for their decisions. This responsibility can be civil, criminal or disciplinary.

Finally, judges are only bound by the law. Judges have a protective status derived from the Constitution and Organic Law of the Judicial Power (Ley Orgánica del Poder Judicial (LOPJ)). As mentioned above, they are irremovable, which means that they cannot be removed, suspended, retired or moved to another place, only in cases specified by the law and according to a particular proceeding. The General Council of the Judiciary controls them.

11. The General Council of the Judiciary is created by the Constitution (Article 122.2) and its functions were established in the law (LOCGPJ, LO 1/80 and LOPJ, amended on several occasions). This Council has different attributions mainly in the appointment of judges (especially the President and other judges of the Supreme Court (Tribunal Supremo (TS)), two judges of the TC, judges of the rest of tribunals, etc.) and informing on matters related to the judicial power. The Council is integrated by the President (who at the same time is the President of the TS), and twenty members, of which ten are elected by the Congress and ten by the Senate. Of the total composition of the Council, twelve members have to be judges and the other eight must have a law degree.

12. The Constitution proclaims the principle of equality in all orders. Equality before justice means that any person has the right to be judged without discrimination and exceptional courts are prohibited by the Constitution (Article 117.6).

13. Justice will be free for those people without economic resources. In those cases, free legal assistance will be provided, in accordance with Law 1/96 (Law of Free Legal Assistance, 'Ley de Asistencia Jurídica Gratuita'). Of course, the parties do not pay the judges; they are civil servants and are paid by the State. Neither do they pay the services of the clerk of the courts who are also civil servants. Only when free legal assistance is provided litigants do not have to pay the fees and expenses of legal advisers. Nevertheless, according to Article 394 NCCP, the judge, in a motivated decision, will impose the cost of the litigation to the losing party, except in exceptional situations.

Law 53/02 of December 30 introduced the need to pay a tax, in some cases, in the civil and administrative courts. Law 10/2012 of November 20 extended the requirement to pay a tax in a greater number of cases. On the contrary, the RD-Law 1/2015 of February 27 exempted natural persons from payment. The TC sentence 140/2016 has to be taken into consideration to determine the amount of money that has to be paid in civil cases.

14. Article 455 NCCP establishes the general principle of the double layer of jurisdiction in civil matters because all judgments in all types of proceedings can be appealed before a Superior Court except in oral proceedings of EUR 3,000 or less. The appeal process is limited under Spanish law. New facts can be brought only in special circumstances, according to Article 460 NCCP and it is not possible to put forward new actions in this second instance.

15. The Spanish Constitution (Constitución Española (CE)) affirms that the civil liberties and fundamental rights have to be interpreted in accordance with the international treaties signed by Spain. For this reason, the European Convention on Human Rights and Fundamental Freedoms is especially important (Treaty of Rome of 4 November 1950, ratified by Spain on 4 October 1979). Article 6 of this Treaty proclaims the following rights:

- The right to a fair trial.
- Proceedings have to be completed in a reasonable time (derecho a un juicio sin dilaciones indebidas). Of course, this right is very difficult to comply with because of the traditional lack of resources in the Spanish judicial system.

- The right to a court established by law.
- The right to an independent and impartial court.
- Publicity of justice, except in some exceptional cases.

Part I. Judicial Organization

Chapter 1. The Courts and Their Members

§1. The Courts

16. In Spain it is necessary to distinguish two types of jurisdiction: constitutional, which is exercised by the TC in certain cases (*see* paragraph 4) and ordinary jurisdiction which corresponds to judges and courts of the so-called judicial power. It is contradictory, but the TC which exercises jurisdiction is not part of the 'judicial power'.

17. The TC, in a certain way, is a special jurisdiction. It is composed of twelve members; the Congress elects four (three-fifth of the votes is required); the Senate elects four (the same majority is needed), the Government chooses two and the General Council of the Judiciary also elects two. The elected members have a nine-year term and every three years one-third of the Court is renewed.

18. As mentioned above in paragraph 4, the ordinary jurisdiction is divided into four areas: civil, criminal, administrative and social or labour.

I. Civil Courts

19. At the first level of the civil court system there are two types of courts: judges of the peace and judges of first instance. The judges of the peace can only deal with very small claims (up to EUR 90). For that reason, the first instance is almost completely managed by the judges of first instance ('jueces de primera instancia'). These judges are distributed all across the country in districts which are called 'partidos judiciales' that are integrated by several municipalities. In the less populated districts there is only one judge of first instance. When the district has a large population there are several judges of first instance, in this case the NCCP and the LOPJ foresee the possibility of specialization of one of the judges in specific matters (family, etc.).

The Organic Law 8/2003 of July 9 established the Commercial Courts as part of the civil jurisdiction. In each province there will be at least one court of this kind. Its main attribute is in bankruptcy matters, but Article 86 *ter* of the LOPJ gave it powers in other areas such as industrial property (trademarks, patents, etc.), intellectual property, maritime law, corporations. One of the Commercial Courts in the province of Alicante has competence in matters of European trademarks. With the reform of LOPJ, bankruptcy of natural persons who are not entrepreneurs shall be the responsibility of the first instance courts.

The Organic Law 1/2004 of 28 December created the so-called Courts for Violence against Women. Their civil powers relate to family issues when there has been an act of violence in the family.

20. In the second level of jurisdiction, acting as courts of appeal, there are the so-called Audiencias Provinciales (Provincial Courts). There is one of these Courts in each one of the provinces. Spain is divided into fifty provinces. In provinces with large populations, the courts are divided into sections to improve their efficiency. Each section is integrated with at least three judges. Originally, the Provincial Courts only dealt with criminal cases, but now they are the ordinary courts of appeal in civil matters. The Provincial Court of Alicante will have at least one section acting as the Community Trademark Appeal Court.

21. As a consequence of the new territorial division imposed by the Constitution, a new type of Court was established in each of the seventeen autonomous regions, namely the Superior Court of Justice. As a civil court (the court also exercises jurisdiction in criminal administrative and social matters), it deals with a new type of appeal introduced by the NCCP. It acts as a court of cassation in matters that only involve the application of laws of the own autonomous region, and it considers lawsuits filed for liability of the members of the regional parliament and Government (Article 73 LOPJ).

22. The TS is divided into five divisions or chambers: civil, criminal, administrative, labour and military. Acting as a civil court, the main purpose of the TS is to unify the interpretation of the law through a special appeal that is called 'recurso de casación'. The TS also deals, among other matters, with motions for review and decides the lawsuits filed for liability of the highest members of the Government, the Parliament and the Judiciary (Article 56 LOPJ).

II. Criminal Courts

23. In order to understand the Spanish criminal court system, it is necessary to say a few words regarding the structure of criminal proceedings in Spain. Traditionally, we had to distinguish between two types of criminal offences: crimes and misdemeanours. For the latter, there is only a single type of trial, the so-called juicio de faltas, but for prosecuting crimes there are four different proceedings: ordinary, 'abreviado' (fast-track trial), 'rapido' (super-fast-track trial) and trial by jury. These four proceedings are divided into two phases: the first is the investigative one ('instrucción o sumario') and the second is the public hearing or trial. Each one of the phases has to be managed by a different court. The proper proceedings to be followed are related with the severity of the punishments to be imposed, except in jury trials. The jury trial is only for the crimes listed in Article 1 of the Organic Law of Jury Trial (Ley Orgánica del Tribunal del Jurado (LOTJ)).

The Organic Law 1/2015 of March 30 amended the Criminal Code and minor offenses are now eliminated. However, trial for misdemeanours remains in effect to judge less serious crimes.

A. *Investigative Judges*

24. Criminal cases, except less serious crimes, have to be investigated by investigative judges. There is at least one investigative judge in each of the districts in which the country is divided ('partidos judiciales' as we said above when we were dealing with the civil court system, paragraph 19). In the small districts, the same judge acts as investigative judge and as judge of first instance, exercising civil and criminal jurisdiction. In cases of violence against women, the investigation is handled by the Judge of Violence against Women.

B. *Criminal Judges*

25. In each province, there is at least one criminal judge to try crimes punishable with up to five years in prison.

C. *Provincial Courts*

26. There is one Provincial Court in each of the fifty provinces of Spain. As stated above, these courts act as civil courts, but they can also try criminal cases. In some crimes they act as a court of instance, in other cases they are courts of appeal, reviewing cases that were tried in first instance by the criminal judges.

D. *Jury Courts*

27. The trial by jury has been reintroduced in Spain by L.O. 5/95, amended by L.O. 8/95 and L.O. 10/95. According to Article 2 L.O. 5/95 nine jurors and two alternate jurors integrate the jury. Usually, a judge of the Provincial Court presides the proceedings. In some cases, the competent court will be the criminal chamber of the Superior Court of Justice or the TS. In those cases, the presiding judge will be a member of the competent court. The jury trial is contemplated for cases of murder, corruption, arson, unlawful entry, embezzlement, etc.

E. *Superior Courts of Justice of Autonomous Regions*

28. The judgment issued after a trial by jury can be appealed to these courts. They act as first instance courts to try crimes of members of the Government and the parliament of the autonomous regions.

F. National Court

29. The National Court was originally created in 1977. This court sits in Madrid and deals with special crimes, such as terrorism, drug-related crimes committed by members of cartels, certain types of economic crimes, etc. These crimes are investigated by the central investigative judges and are tried by the central criminal judges or the criminal division of the national court, depending on the punishment foreseen by the law. The judgment can be appealed to the Appeal Chamber of the National Court.

G. The Supreme Court

30. The competence of the criminal division of the TS is very important: Cassation and trial of the crimes committed by the members of the Government, parliament and other high officials.

III. Administrative Courts

31. In Spain, administrative courts control the activity of the Government and the Public Administration when they are acting according to administrative law. The courts are organized as follows:

A. Administrative Judges

32. Each province has at least one administrative judge. The jurisdiction of these judges is exercised in certain matters of the municipalities, autonomous communities and Central Government.

B. Superior Court of Justice of the Autonomous Communities

33. They act as courts of appeal and as courts of first instance, especially when it is a matter related to the application of norms that have its origin within their own autonomous community.

C. National Court

34. The administrative division of the National Court controls certain acts of the Central Government in cases where the competent authority is a high official of the Government. There are also central judges in the administrative division.

D. Supreme Court

35. The TS acts as a cassation court, but it is also a first instance court when the act to be controlled has its origin in the Cabinet.

IV. Labour Courts

A. Labour Judges

36. There is at least one labour judge in each province. They are first instance judges in labour and social security cases.

B. Superior Court of the Autonomous Communities

37. The labour division of the Superior Court of the autonomous communities deals with a special appeal in labour matters which is called 'suplicación' and they are also first instance courts in certain matters.

C. National Court

38. The labour division of the National Court exercises its jurisdiction as a first instance court in matters related to contracts between employers and employees when it is a contract that has to be applied in the territory of more than one autonomous community.

D. Supreme Court

39. The labour division of the TS has a very similar role in labour matters as the one that exercises jurisdiction in civil cases.

40. There are others courts in Spain such as juvenile courts and judges that control the enforcement of the punishment in criminal cases. Of course, the military has its own courts. There are also the so-called traditional courts: Tribunal de las Aguas in Valencia and Consejo de Hombres Buenos de Murcia, that deal with the problems related to the use of water for agricultural purposes. Finally, we have to consider the existence of supranational courts: The European Court of Human Rights and the Court of Justice of the European Communities.

§2. Members of the Courts

I. Judges

41. There are different methods to become a member of the judicial career, as stated in the LOPJ:

(1) A method most often used in recruiting judges is through a national examination. After taking part and passing the examination there is a period of practice in the school of judges. When the judges finish school they are usually appointed to a first instance court.
(2) The second way to become a judge is by taking part in a contest among jurists with more than ten years of experience. After being selected on merits (e.g., law degrees, seniority in their career as public servants, courses, articles and books written) they are usually appointed to a first instance court or a Court of Appeals. They must attend a training course at the Judicial School.
(3) The third way is by taking part in a contest among jurists with more than fifteen years of experience. After being selected on merits they become 'judges of the Supreme Court'.
(4) The fourth and final method is a very special way to become a judge in the civil/criminal division of the Superior Court of Justice of the Autonomous Communities. Each autonomous parliament presents a list of three members to the General Council of the Judiciary and they select one.

42. There are three categories in the judicial career which will be described from bottom to top:

(1) Judges.
(2) Magistrates: There are two methods to become a magistrate:
    (a) First by seniority (at least three years as a judge).
    (b) Second by taking part in specialization courses and examinations.
(3) Magistrates of the TS: The magistrates of the TS are appointed by the General Council of the Judiciary taking into account seniority greater than fifteen years in the judicial career.

43. One of the most important guarantees of the judges is their independence. This implies that the law regulates a series of conditions to guarantee their independence:

(1) Conditions to become a member:
    (a) Spanish citizenship.
    (b) Legal age (majority of age).
    (c) Law degree.
    (d) People who have physical or psychological impairments cannot become a member of the judicial career and neither can anyone who has been sentenced or indicted on certain crimes.

(2) Prohibitions or incompatibilities:
   (a) The judicial career is incompatible with the exercise of another public function.
   (b) It is also incompatible with having a job in the public or private sector with the exception of academic or artistic jobs.
   (c) They cannot work as attorneys or as a person who represents a party in a trial.
   (d) They cannot give paid or free counsel.
   (e) They cannot be executives of public or private corporations.
   (f) They cannot be members of political parties or unions.
   (g) There are also certain provisions regarding family ties.

(3) Irremovability:
   – This is the right of the judges not to be removed, suspended, moved or retired only by the causes indicated in the law.
   – Judges can only be removed by the causes specified in Article 379 LOPJ. They can only be suspended by the causes contained in Article 383 LOPJ.
   – We have to distinguish between temporary suspension and definite removal.
   – According to LOPJ a move to another location is voluntary, but exceptionally it can happen that a mandatory move is required as a disciplinary action as specified by law.

Retirement can only occur for two causes:

(1) Age, when the judge turns seventy years old. The LOPJ, after its modification, allows a request for retirement at the age of seventy-two.
(2) Permanent physical or psychological impairment, but in this case only after a contradictory proceeding.

44. Duties and rights:

(1) Duties: The main duty of the judge is to judge in a fair and impartial way. The law requires that a judge must reside in the city where the court has its seat. The law also requires that the judge complies with a schedule and other requirements stated in Articles 417–419 LOPJ.
(2) Rights: We have to distinguish between ordinary rights and what the law considers special rights:
   – Ordinary rights: Judges have the right to be paid, to take leaves of absence, to be promoted, etc.
   – Among the Special rights we can highlight two:
      (a) The right to become a member of a professional association.
      (b) The so-called immunity that specifically means that a judge can only be arrested by a court order or if a judge is in the act of committing a crime. (Articles 398–400 LOPJ).
(3) Liabilities: Judges are subject to criminal and disciplinary actions. The disciplinary actions are stated in Article 420 LOPJ and consist of the following: Warnings, fines, mandatory move and permanent removal. The LOPJ has

removed the direct civil liability of judges, but the State can claim reimbursement of the compensation paid to parties for damages caused by judges.

Chapter 2. The Bar

45. Becoming a member of the bar is very simple. The only prerequisites are:

- Spanish citizenship or of one of the countries of the European Union.
- You must be of legal age.
- You must have a law degree.
- No previous criminal record.
- You must pay an admission fee.
- You must pay a special tax.

46. Law 34/2006 of October 30 sets new prerequisites in order to join a Bar Association requiring specialized training (a master's in Law is required) and passing an entrance examination. Law 34/2006 came into effect in November 2011.

Before Law 7/97, it was necessary to be a member of the bar of the court where the lawyer wanted to practice. After that law came into effect, you were allowed to be a member of the bar anywhere and you were allowed work anywhere in the country.

After becoming a member of the bar, the General Statute of Lawyers (Estatuto General de la Abogacía (EGA)) (RD 658/2001, June 22) regulates the duties of the lawyer with the bar, with their colleagues, with the courts and with the parties. There are also norms regarding the professional fees and the so-called turno de oficio (free legal counsel).

47. Lawyers have to be protected by the courts in their right to speak and their right to defend. They have to act according to the bona fide principle and they have the right to collect professional fees ('honorarios'). These fees are freely negotiated between the lawyer and the client and are based on the difficulty of the case and the criteria of the attorney. Nevertheless, the bar usually has norms to guide the charging of fees. It is very important to underline that the so-called *quota litis* is prohibited (but it is commonly used). The TS, Administrative Chamber, has declared that the contingency fee is admitted into our law (Resolution of 4 November 2008).

48. Attorneys are bound by professional secrecy. An attorney has limited rights to publicity and the profession is incompatible with the exercise of another profession except in the case of teaching which is admissible.

49. The attorneys are subject to disciplinary proceedings in case of professional misconduct. These proceedings are held before the bar that he or she belongs to and the proceedings are adversary. The decisions of the bar on disciplinary matters can be appealed to the 'Consejo General de la Abogacía' (General Council of Lawyers) and subsequently the administrative jurisdiction.

Lawyers are subject to either civil or criminal proceedings in case of wrongdoing when practising their profession.

50. Traditionally, the bars have assumed the free defence of people without financial resources and for that purpose the 'turno de oficio' lists were created. This duty was originally without pay but now it is subsidized with public funds, however, not at the same rate as the market.

51. The bars are subject to public regulations. EGA promotes provincial bars but the old small district bars continue to exist if they have at least ten lawyers residing in the district. The EGA does not promote the creation of new bars.

The bar has the following objectives: To defend the professional interests of the lawyers, to represent and to keep order in the exercise of the profession and to cooperate with the courts.

52. As we have said earlier, it is necessary to be a member of the bar to become an attorney, but the bars cannot limit the number of people who want to join. Since the entry into force of Law 34/2006, however, candidate attorneys must pass a bar examination.

53. The organization of the bar has the following structure:

- 'Decano'. The Dean represents the bar and presides over all the meetings of the bar. He or she is an elected person.
- 'Junta de Gobierno'. This is the governing body of the bar. It is also elected by all the members of the bar and is composed of a Dean, a Secretary, a Treasurer, a librarian and a number of representatives no less than two and no more than twelve.
- 'Junta General'. In this general meeting all members of the bar can participate.

The 'Consejo General de la Abogacia' is a coordinating body of all bars in Spain and finally the Deans Assembly is the supreme body of this legal profession in Spain.

Chapter 3. Other Legal Professions Intervening in Civil Proceedings

§1. PRIVATE

I. 'Procuradores'

54. 'Procuradores' are professional legal people that represent the parties before the courts. Except in some cases, the attorney is not authorized to represent his or her client, because the monopoly of representation belongs to the 'procuradores'. In other words, the attorney defends and the 'procurador' represents. As mentioned above, this function is compulsory and exclusive. Article 23 of NCCP says that the party has to be represented before a court by a 'procurador' in all cases except in the following:

- Oral trials of less than EUR 2,000 and for the initial petition in the so-called proceso monitorio.
- In bankruptcy cases where the party only wants to appear in court to present himself as a creditor or only wants to attend to creditors meetings.
- In some proceedings regarding free legal advice and when the party is asking for pretrial proceedings.

55. The exclusiveness of the function of the 'procurador' means that no other person can represent the parties, only when specially authorized by law. Usually, the law does not authorize other persons to represent the parties except in labour and social security proceedings.

56. The law requires that the contract between the party and the 'procurador' be in writing before a public notary or before the court. The law (Article 25 NCCP) distinguishes between general and special representation. Usually, the general representation contract is enough but in some cases the law requires a special representation agreement.

57. The relationship between the party and the 'procurador' is based on trust. This is more of a theoretical situation than a real one because it is very common that the party contracts the 'procurador' that the attorney recommends. Therefore, in reality, the trust is based on the relationship with the lawyer.

58. The 'procuradores' must also be members of a bar. To become a member, it is necessary to comply with the following requisites:

- Spanish citizenship or any of the European Union countries.
- To be of legal age.
- To have a law degree.
- To make a bond.
- To make an oath.

Law 34/2006 is also applicable to the 'procuradores'.

59. The fees that the 'procurador' has a right to collect are called 'aranceles' (scales) and they are fixed.

60. The 'procuradores' bar is also subject to public law and there is usually a bar in each province but smaller bars can exist.

The bar is organized as follows:

- A dean who represents the bar and presides over all meetings.
- 'Junta de Gobierno' which is integrated by the Dean, Secretary, Treasurer and other elected members.
- 'Junta General' composed by all the members of the bar.

The 'Consejo General de los Ilustres Colegios de los Procuradores de los Tribunales de Espana' coordinates all the bars of Spain.

61. The 'procurador' may also be subject to disciplinary proceedings before the bar. Civil and criminal proceedings are also possible.

§2. Public

I. 'Letrados de la Administración de Justicia' (Deputy Clerks)

62. Each court must have a 'letrado de la Administración de Justicia'. The Organic Law 7/2015 of July 21 replaced the name 'Secretario Judicial' for 'Letrado de la Administración de Justicia'. Under the first additional provision of the Act, all references in earlier legislation made to 'Secretario Judicial' must be understood to be made to 'Letrados de la Administración de Justicia'.

This public official has the following functions among others:

- acting as a public notary in the judicial proceeding.
- being the personnel manager of the court.
- bearing responsibility for the custody of documents, objects and money of the legal proceedings.
- maintaining the statistical records of the court.

Law 13/2009 of November 3 has significantly increased the powers of the Deputy Clerks, who are entrusted during the proceedings with a number of procedural issues, such as initial control of the procedural requirements, determination of the day of the hearing (in accordance with the judge's instructions), increased responsibility in execution proceedings, resolving disputes of legal costs of proceedings.

63. The 'secretarios judiciales' are members of a legal public career and they are organized as follows:

- First category: TS and certain jobs in the National court and Superior Court of Justice of the autonomous communities.
- Second Category: National Court, Superior Court of Justice, Provincial Courts and certain jobs in first instance courts.
- Third Category: first instance courts.

64. There are two ways to become a 'Secretario Judicial.' First, by taking part in a national examination and after passing the examination there is a period of practice; second, by taking part in a contest among personnel that work for the administration of justice and after being selected there is also a period of practice. They are subject to almost the same incompatibilities and prohibitions as the judges. They are dependent on the Ministry of Justice and they have to be independent and impartial. As legal servants they are paid directly by the State and not by any of the parties. A law degree is always required.

II. 'Oficiales, Auxiliares, Agentes Judiciales'

65. 'Oficiales, Auxiliares, Agentes Judiciales' (Organic Law 19/2003 now refers to them as 'cuerpo de gestión procesal y administrativo' – procedural management and administrative body; 'cuerpo de tramitacion procesal y administrativo' – proceedings and administrative body; and 'cuerpo de auxilio judicial – legal aid body) are legal servants that work in the judicial office under the direct supervision of the 'Secretario Judicial'. Their duties are varied: Notifications to the parties, substitution of the 'secretario', evictions, seizures, etc.

Currently, these employees work together in the so-called judicial offices which are basically divided into two classes: those who provide direct support to one judicial body and those who provide 'common services' for several judicial bodies.

III. Public Attorneys: 'Ministerio Fiscal'

66. According to Article 124 of the CE the Public Attorney has to defend the law, citizens' rights and has to watch over the independence of the courts and must procure the satisfaction of the social interests before the courts. Keeping in mind these functions, the role of the Public Attorney in civil proceedings is very limited except when the public interest is involved, like in cases of personal status, and when representing minors or people who are absent.

67. The Public Attorneys are regulated in the Constitution, LOPJ, and basically in the 'Estatuto Orgánico del Ministerio Fiscal' (Law 50/81, 30 December).

The Public Attorney is not a part of the judicial power because he does not exercise jurisdiction and he is not integrated in the organization of the courts.

68. The Public Attorneys' office is organized in several bodies and the main one is the Attorney General who is officially appointed by the King but who is really chosen by the Government. The law requires that this person has more than fifteen years of law practice.

The Public Attorneys' office works under the principle of unity and hierarchy. The first means that there is only one Public Attorney organization in Spain and the second implies that the organization has a top-to-bottom structure and the superior organs can give direct orders and instructions to the inferior ones. On the other hand, the Public Attorney must act subject to the law and according to the principle of impartiality.

The members of the Public Attorneys' office (all except the Attorney General who is not necessarily a public servant) are public servants and their career is organized in three categories: First, Public Attorneys in the TS; second, 'fiscales'; and third, 'abogados fiscales'. To become a member, it is necessary to take part in and pass a national examination. A law degree is always required.

In conclusion, the Public Attorneys' office is characterized for not being part of the judicial power and for being the legal expression of the policy of the Government mainly the criminal policy.

IV. 'Abogados del Estado'

69. This Government body has its origin in the defence of property of the State and its functions today are the representation and defence of the State in all kinds of proceedings, but mostly in the administrative jurisdiction.

The Autonomous Communities usually have its own lawyers to represent and defend them before the courts but it is also possible that the Communities use the services of the 'abogados del estado'.

Finally, the municipalities can have its own lawyers or they can hire a private lawyer to defend them before the courts in a specific case.

Part II. Jurisdiction

Chapter 1. Domestic Jurisdiction

70. Previously, we referred to the different types of courts when we outlined the Spanish Jurisdictional Organization. Furthermore, we explained the existence of specialized jurisdictions each with its own courts. In referring to the civil jurisdiction, we will review the attributes of each of the bodies that exercise jurisdiction of civil order.

§1. Subject Matter Jurisdiction

I. Judges of the Peace

71. The Courts of the Peace examine those cases that do not exceed EUR 90 (Article 47 NCCP) and they exclude those matters that are referred to in Article 250.1 NCCP.

II. First Instance Courts

72. First instance courts examine all civil matters that, due to legal dispositions, have not been assigned to other courts. Furthermore, they will review matters, acts and other questions that the LOPJ attributes to it.

III. Commercial Courts

73. Its main attribute is in bankruptcy matters, but Article 86 *ter* of the LOPJ gave it powers in other areas such as industrial property (trademarks, patents, etc.), intellectual property, maritime law, corporations.

The Organic Law 7/2015 of July 15, Article 86.6 in force since 1 October 2015, states that bankruptcy proceedings of a non-entrepreneurial natural person will be the competence of the Court of First Instance and not the Commercial Courts.

IV. Courts for Violence against Women

74. Their civil powers relate to family issues when there has been an act of violence in the family.

V. Provincial Courts

75. The Provincial Courts act mainly as courts of appeal in civil matters.

VI. Superior Courts of Justice of the Autonomous Communities

76. The civil/criminal chamber of the Superior Court of Justice will examine, as a civil chamber, liability suits filed against the President and members of the Government body of the Autonomous Community and against members of the Legislative Assembly for acts committed while exercising his or her functions. There are cases which the jurisdiction corresponds to the TS when the Statute of Autonomy has that provision. Furthermore, it will examine the liability suits against all or most of the magistrates of the Provincial Courts or any of its sections for acts committed while exercising his or her functions.

VII. Supreme Court

77. The civil division of the TS will examine the liability suits filed against any of the following persons while in the act of exercising his or her functions: President of the Government, President of Congress, President of the Senate, President of the TS, President of the TC, Members of the Cabinet, Congressmen, Senators, Members of the General Council of the Judicial Power, Justices of the TS and TC, President of the National Court, President of the Superior Courts of Justice and its divisions, Attorney General, Public Attorneys acting before the TS, President and members of the State Audit Court, Ombudsman and President and Members of the Cabinet of the Autonomous Communities in those cases in which the statute of autonomy establishes this provision.

Furthermore, it will examine those liability suits filed against judges of the National Court and Superior Courts of Justice for acts committed while carrying out his or her functions.

Finally, the TS examines the suits asking the recognition and enforcement of foreign decisions only when it is established in international treaties.

We must remember that all labour matters (salaries, unfair dismissal, etc.) and social security matters are not under civil jurisdiction but under labour courts.

§2. Venue (Territorial Jurisdiction)

78. The first rule established by the NCCP (Article 54) to determine territorial jurisdiction in a specific case is an agreement between the parties. This possibility has numerous exceptions and is prohibited in adhesion contracts and contracts involving the rights of consumers. The agreement may be of two types: (1) explicit and (2) presumed. It is explicit when the parties involved clearly indicate which will be the court where their disputes will be heard (Article 55 NCCP). It is a presumed agreement when the plaintiff files suit in a Court and the defendant does not object (Article 56).

If the parties involved do not agree, the rules contained in Articles 50–53 of the NCCP will apply.

79. As general criterion the court instituted corresponds to the place of domicile of the defendant and if a domicile is not available the place of residence is used. If a domicile or residence is not available within Spain, a suit may be filed against the defendant in any location where he or she is found within Spain or at the place of last residence. If none of the previous rules apply, the suit will be filed in the court corresponding to the domicile of the plaintiff (Article 50.2 NCCP). Jurisdiction of suits against companies will take place at the corporate headquarters existing additional complementary criteria conferring competence.

80. Nevertheless, in special cases a number of rules exist to establish territorial jurisdiction. The main ones are as follows:

- In immovable property cases, the jurisdiction will take place at the location of the property.
- In cases involving hereditary matters, jurisdiction corresponds to the place where the deceased was domiciled. If he or she was domiciled in a foreign country, the claimant may decide between the deceased's last domicile in Spain or where the majority of his assets are located.
- The cases involving representation or assistance for disabled people, jurisdiction applies to the court where the person resides.
- In cases that involve protecting fundamental rights, jurisdiction corresponds to the place where the plaintiff is domiciled. If the plaintiff's domicile is in a foreign country, jurisdiction will take place where his or her fundamental rights were violated.
- In trials involving rental properties and evictions, jurisdiction corresponds to the place where the property is located.
- In matters that involve accidents with motor vehicles, jurisdiction for compensation of civil damages will take place where the incident occurred.
- Cases which object to decisions of the organs of the legal persons and companies jurisdiction will take place where the company has its seat.
- In any lawsuit which involves infringement of intellectual property, the claimant may choose between the jurisdiction of the court where the violation has occurred or is presumed to have taken place or where the illegal copies were found.

81. According to Spanish law (as stated in LOPJ and the Organic Law of Jurisdiction Conflicts, LO 2/87, May 18), the conflicts of jurisdiction can be of four types:

(1) Conflicts between jurisdiction and administration, which are called 'conflictos de atribuciones'. These conflicts are solved by a special court (Tribunal de Conflictos de Jurisdicción). This court has a unique composition (Article 38 LOPJ and Article 1 LO 2/87). It is integrated by three members of the Council of State (representing administration) and three members of the TS, of which one is the President of the TS who has a deciding vote in case of a draw among the members of this special court.

The conflicts between administration and jurisdiction can be of two types: Positive conflicts (jurisdiction and administration consider a particular case is by law attributed to their organs) and negative conflicts (neither jurisdiction nor administration considers that the case when they are requested to act by somebody is by law attributed to them).

The proceedings to solve these conflicts are in Articles 3–21 of LO 2/87. In its judgment the deciding court ('Tribunal de Conflictos' as we said above) shall decide if jurisdiction or administration has the competence. This judgment can be appealed to the TC if a party considers that a fundamental right has been violated.

(2) The second type of conflict can oppose the courts of ordinary jurisdiction and the courts of the military jurisdiction (Conflictos de jurisdicción). This conflict is decided by a special court, which, according to Article 22 LO 2/87 and Article 39 LOPJ, is called the chamber of conflicts of jurisdiction (Sala de Conflictos de Jurisdicción). It is integrated by five members. One is the President of the TS, two are members of the military chamber of the TS and the other two are members of the chamber of the TS which is in conflict with the military chamber, usually the criminal chamber. The conflicts can also be positive or negative and the proceedings are the same as we stated above for the first type of conflict.

(3) The third type of conflict can oppose courts of the ordinary jurisdiction (e.g., a civil court and a labour court). They are called 'conflictos de competencia'. The conflict is decided by a special chamber of the TS: The President of the TS and a member of the chambers in conflict. This type of conflict can also be positive or negative and proceedings are in Articles 43–50 LOPJ.

(4) Finally, there is a fourth type of conflict between courts of the same jurisdiction (e.g., two judges of first instance). In this case the conflict (i.e., called 'cuestiones de competencia') is decided by the court which is the immediate Superior Court to both.

Chapter 2. International Jurisdiction

82. Article 21 LOPJ states that Spanish Courts have jurisdiction in all cases which arise in Spanish territory in accordance with international treaties signed by Spain, as per the rules of the European Union and the Spanish laws. This rule respects the immunities of jurisdiction and enforcement of the States set in the Convention of Vienna of 18 April 1961. The TC said in its judgment of 28 September 1995 that those immunities do not infringe the constitutional rights that are established in Article 24 of the CE.

83. If there is no international treaty or European law applicable, the rules for establishing Spanish jurisdiction are laid down in Article 22 to Article 22 *septies* LOPJ. These articles set the jurisdiction of the Spanish civil courts according to the following criteria:

(a) General criteria: Spanish civil courts will have jurisdiction when there is an agreement between the parties to bring the case before Spanish Courts. Such agreement can be presumed if the plaintiff chooses a Spanish Court and the defendant does not object. Spanish civil courts may also hear a case when the defendant appears before the court and the jurisdiction is not contested.
(b) Exclusive jurisdiction: Spanish civil courts shall have exclusive jurisdiction in the following cases:
   - In proceedings which have as their object rights in rem in immovable property or tenancies of immovable property when Spain is where the property is situated.
   - In proceedings which have as their object the validity of the Constitution, the nullity or the dissolution of companies or other legal persons, or the decisions of their organs, when the companies or legal persons or association have their seat in Spain.
   - In proceedings which have as their object the validity of entries in Spanish public registers.
   - In proceedings concerned with the registration of validity of patents, trademarks, designs or other similar rights required to be deposited or registered, when the deposit or registration has been applied for in Spain.
   - In proceedings concerned with the enforcement of judgment when the judgment has to be enforced in Spain.
(c) Special jurisdiction: Articles 22 quater to *septies* LOPJ establish a great number of cases that allow Spanish Courts to exercise its jurisdiction when the previous cases of (a) and (b) do not apply.

Part III. Actions and Claims

Chapter 1. Actions

§1. Definition

84. In Spanish law there is no definition for 'action'. Nevertheless, it is clear that an action is something different from a subjective right and that it is a right in itself.

Two basic types of actions have to be considered: Declarative actions and actions for the enforcement of judgments. In the first case, the action is focused on the declaration of a subjective right. In the second case, the purpose of the action is the enforcement of a right based on a judgment, a deed or other type of document.

It is also clear that the word action is used in a different way when it is equivalent to a substantive right as it is used *per exemplum* in '*actio reivindicatoria*', '*actio ex contractu*', '*actio ex delicto*', etc.

§2. Admissibility of an Action

85. Under Spanish law, there is no rule for the admissibility of actions but of the claims. According to Article 403.1 of the NCCP, the general norm is that every claim is admissible except if otherwise stated by the law.

§3. Interest to Sue

86. The interest to sue is not defined by law, but it is necessary to have a legitimate one. Interest is the benefit that the plaintiff will gain if the judgment is favourable to him or her. The concept of 'legitimated' interest is not defined either, but Article 7 of the Civil Code (Código Civil (CC)) states that the law does not protect the abuse or the antisocial use of a right. A claim that is contrary to the law or public policy is not admissible.

The interest to sue must be proven when the party is exercising declarative or constitutive actions.

Exceptionally, the law prohibits the exercise of a right through an action. It is the case of the promise of marriage (Article 42 CC). In case of breaching that promise, the party can only sue for an amount of money to compensate the expenses caused.

§4. Collective Actions

87. Article 11 of the NCCP foresees three types of collective actions:

(a) Actions brought before a court by associations for the protection of consumer rights, the Public Attorney or, in some cases, unions.
(b) Actions by a group of consumers that have suffered a damage and where the people are fully identified.
(c) Actions by a group of consumers that have suffered a damage and where the people are not fully identified.

§5. Vexatious Litigation

88. Article 11 of LOPJ states that the courts will not protect actions or ancillary actions that imply abuse of a right, bad faith, fraudulent use of a right or abuse of process. Furthermore, Article 247.3 NCCP reads that the courts can impose a fine of up to EUR 6,000 to the party acting in a vexatious way (with a limit of one-third of the amount of the claim). To determine the fine, the court will have to take into consideration the factual circumstances and the damages caused. If the court thinks that a lawyer, or a representative, is responsible for the act against good faith he will be fined and the bar will be informed. The bar will decide if disciplinary proceedings are necessary.

Chapter 2. Claims and Defences

§1. Claims

89. According to Article 399 NCCP the proceedings will begin with the claim. The form of the claim is as follows:

(a) Identification of the plaintiff and his/her domicile and identification of his/her attorney and 'procurador'.
(b) Identification of the defendant and his/her address (domicile or residence) where the writ of summons has to be served.
(c) Identification of factual background. The facts have to be stated in a precise and clear manner in order to facilitate the defendant's admittance or denial of the facts.
(d) Law applicable to the case. There are two types of law pleadings: (i) law regarding the object of the proceedings or substantive law and (ii) law applicable to procedural matters (sometimes improperly called adjective law): capacity, representation, jurisdiction, competence, type of proceeding, etc.
(e) Relief that it is sought. If the plaintiff is requesting relief in several matters they have to be stated separately.

90. Article 387 NCCP refers to ancillary claims. An ancillary claim is a claim presented in the course of a proceeding already initiated. It is different from the main object but is related to it.

Ancillary claims are also those that are referred to procedural requirements of influence in the due course of the proceedings.

Considering other points of view, ancillary claims can be of:

(a) special decision. They are decided separately from the main claim;
(b) previous decision. They have to be resolved prior to the main object.

§2. Defence

91. The defence is the answer of the defendant to the claim of the plaintiff. According to Articles 405 and 438 of the NCCP, the defence will have the same form as the claim. In oral proceedings the defence was a verbal exposition at the beginning of the trial, except in special cases such as divorce, but now it is always a written document according to the modification of Article 438 NCCP made by Law 42/2015 of October 5.

The defendant can take different attitudes towards the claim. In the first place, the defendant can oppose procedural exceptions. According to Article 416 NCCP the main procedural exceptions are:

– Lack of capacity or representation.
– Res judicata.

- *Lis pendens.*
- Compulsory joinder of co-defendants.
- Inadequate proceedings.
- Legal defect in the form of the claim.

Second, the defendant can use a defence based on the merits. A defence on the merits is a plea opposing the truth of the plaintiff's case. This defence can be in different ways:

- Denial of the facts stated by the plaintiff.
- The defendant raises new facts and offers new evidence to avoid a judgment against him. Obviously, he has the burden of proof of the new facts.
- The defendant agrees on the facts, but denies the legal consequences alleged by the plaintiff.
- The defendant introduces new facts that are not necessarily incompatible with the facts alleged by the plaintiff, but in case they are true the claim has to be rejected.
- Counterclaim. Finally, the defendant can introduce a counterclaim. Counterclaims are not a mere defence or denial, but are the introduction of another cause of action. Counterclaim is foreseen in Article 406 of NCCP. It has to be presented in the same way as the claim and it has to be related with the main object of the claim. NCCP does not permit independent or separated counterclaims, as did the Old Code of Civil Procedure (Ley de Enjuiciamiento Civil de 1881 (LEC)). There are several rules that the defendant has to respect: The judge has to be competent and the type of proceedings has to be the same.

Under Spanish law, the general rule is that if the claim is presented in a legal and proper form it has to be admitted. Demurrers, meaning that the pleading of the plaintiff does not state a cause of action or general demurrer, are exceptional and are only permitted when the law specifically admits them.

Chapter 3. Sanctions and Procedural Irregularities

92. Procedural irregularities are defined in Articles 238–243 LOPJ and Articles 225–252 NCCP.

The legal regulation distinguishes between nullity and irregularity. There are two types of nullity: Absolute and relative. Articles 238 LOPJ and 225 NCCP states that a proceeding will be null and void in the following cases:

- When the court has no jurisdiction or competence.
- When the procedural act has been made under violence or intimidation.
- When a procedural act has been made without following compulsory legal rules or without respecting the basic principles of the proceedings, for example the right to be heard, the right to counsel. In these cases, the party has to prove that there has been a real prejudice.
- When conducted without an attorney, in cases which the law establishes it as obligatory.
- When hearings take place without the required intervention of the deputy clerk.
- When the deputy clerk decides matters that the law requires to be solved by the Court.
- In the rest of the cases in which this law so provides.

Article 243 LOPJ states that an act is relatively null when it has been made without all the legal requirements.

The court ex officio or the parties using different types of review proceedings can request absolute nullity.

Part IV. Proceedings

Chapter 1. Pretrial Proceedings

§1. Conciliation

93. There are several ways to avoid a civil trial. One of these is conciliation. According to Article 139 of Law 15/2015, Law of Voluntary Jurisdiction, a party can try conciliation except for the following cases:

(a) When the defendant will be the Government of the State, of the autonomous regions or, in general, the Public Administration.
(b) In matters referring to persons who are not of legal age or when they do not have legal capacity to manage their property.
(c) In cases of civil liability of judges.
(d) Generally speaking, when the object of the future proceeding is not of free disposition to the parties.

Conciliation is a very simple proceeding. It begins when somebody presents a written document asking to summon the future defendant before him. There will be a public hearing which will try to conciliate the parties. If conciliation is reached, this agreement is equivalent to a judgment rendered by a court.

Conciliation proceedings can be brought before the clerk of the Court of First Instance, Commercial Courts or the Judge of the Peace.

§2. Preliminary Proceedings

94. Sometimes, it is necessary to use the preliminary proceedings to know something relevant for the future trial. Therefore, the plaintiff can ask the future defendant about his/her capacity, representation or standing. In the same way, the defendant can ask the plaintiff to show property or other things. In cases referring to testaments and last wills the defendant can be asked to show the document in which the last will is stated. Every partner of a company can ask for the exhibition of documents or the balance. In cases of insurance, the plaintiff can ask the defendant to show the insurance policy and, finally, in cases regarding the protection of consumer rights, the future plaintiff can ask the court to help him determine the people affected by requesting the cooperation of the future defendant. All the costs and expenses caused by these proceedings will be paid for by the future plaintiff and he must also post a bond to cover possible damages. (Article 256 NCCP).

The first instance judge or Commercial Courts of the domicile of the future defendant is the competent court in these proceedings. (Article 257 NCCP).

Chapter 2. Proceedings in First Instance

§1. Adversary Proceedings

I. Ordinary Proceedings

A. Principles Governing a Lawsuit

95. The NCCP presents the common rules to all proceedings in the first book; in the second book, rules to declarative proceedings are presented and in the third book the rules to enforce judgments. The principle of the parties' initiative is affirmed in Article 216 NCCP, but there are a few cases in which the case is not governed by the adversarial principle (capacity, maternity, paternity and, with some peculiarities, divorce). The judge is bound by the parties' demand and cannot decide issues beyond what is claimed, but must decide on everything that is claimed (Article 228 NCCP).

According to Article 282 NCCP facts have to be proven by the parties, but the judge can intervene according to the rules governing evidence. The court can examine the parties (Article 306); it can ask questions to parties or witnesses or questions to clarify the testimony of expert witnesses (Article 347); it can inspect property, things and persons for itself (Articles 353–357), etc.

The judge has to decide according to the petitions of the parties, but he or she is not bound by the law put forward by the parties, because of the rules in the Latin maxim '*iura novit curia*' (Article 218.1 NCCP). The principle of adversary procedure is also stated in Article 24 of the CE.

B. Ordinary Proceedings

96. Under Spanish Law, there are two main types of ordinary proceedings: The so-called ordinary (juicio ordinario) and oral proceedings (juicio verbal). The first one has to be used when the value of the claim is more than EUR 6,000, and it is also used in the cases prescribed in Article 249 NCCP. The second proceeding must be used in claims with a value of less than EUR 6,000 and also in the cases stated in Article 250 NCCP.

1. Introduction of the Claim in Ordinary Proceedings

97. Proceedings in first instance begin when the plaintiff brings his claim before the court (Article 398 NCCP). If the claim is presented according to the law, the clerk will examine the law suit and it is accepted if it meets all the requirements. Otherwise, the Court will be notified. The judge ex officio controls his own jurisdiction and competence and after that he will summon the defendant to appear before the court and to present his defence in twenty days. The writ of summons will be served in the defendant's domicile as is stated in the claim (Article 155 NCCP). If the domicile is unknown, the plaintiff will ask the court to help him to find it. (Article 156 NCCP).

If the defendant does not appear before the court in twenty days, he or she will be declared in default. When the defendant brings his or her defence within that period, one of the things that he or she can do is introducing a counterclaim which means that both parties are plaintiff and defendant, at the same time. The counterclaim has to be presented in the same form as the claim. The court has to control its jurisdiction and competence and both actions (claim and counterclaim) have to be related.

2. Preliminary Hearing

98. After the introduction of the defence, the clerk will summon both parties to a preliminary hearing (audiencia previa al juicio). This hearing has several purposes (Articles 414–430 NCCP):

(a) First of all, the judge will ask the parties if a settlement can be reached. If there is such a settlement, the proceedings will end.
(b) If the settlement is not reached, the court will examine if there are procedural exceptions such as lack of capacity or representation, res judicata, *lis pendens*, *exceptio pluris litisconsortium*, inadequate proceedings, legal defect in the form of the claim or counter claim.

It is not possible to control the lack of jurisdiction or competence by the defendant at this moment, because this matter was previously controlled through 'declinatoria', but the judge can determine if he or she has jurisdiction of competence ex officio.

In this hearing, additional pleadings can be made and they can add complementary petitions but without altering the main object of the claim or counterclaim. In the same way, they can introduce new facts.

In this hearing, each party has to say whether he or she admits the documents presented by the other as valid. If they think that a document is not authentic, they must introduce evidence about its authenticity.

Likewise, the parties must say which facts are certain and which are uncertain. At this very moment, taking into account the whole situation, the court can ask the parties again if a settlement is possible.

If the parties agree on the facts, the judge will decide the case without evidence proceedings. But if a settlement was not reached and the parties disagree about the facts, the court will ask the parties what evidence they want to introduce in the proceedings. The court then decides over the admissibility of the requested evidence. The clerk has to set up the day of the trial, except when documents are the only admissible evidence.

3. The Trial

99. The trial's main purpose is to introduce evidence (Articles 431–433 NCCP). The lawyers have to attend the trial. Once the evidence has been introduced, the parties can allege their final conclusions and they have to summarize the facts which, according to their view, they consider as true. Finally, they will express the points of law which, in their opinion, are applicable to the facts.

4. Oral Proceedings

100. In the case of an oral proceeding the so-called juicio verbal (Articles 437–447 NCCP) will start with a claim with the same requisites as a claim in ordinary proceedings. It is also possible, when the intervention of attorneys and 'procuradores' is not required (i.e., when the amount of the claim is less than EUR 2,000), to begin with the so-called succinct or concise claim in which the exposition of facts and points of law is not required and an application form will be available and the plaintiff only has to fill in the blank spaces. If the defendant wants to introduce a counterclaim, it will only be admissible if this claim is connected with the claim introduced by the plaintiff. The plaintiff can answer the counterclaim in ten days.

The court, after examining its own jurisdiction and competence, will decide the admissibility of the claim. The parties must state whether or not they consider a hearing necessary. If neither party request it, and the court does not consider it necessary a judgment will be rendered without further procedures. Otherwise, the clerk will set up a date for the hearing. If the plaintiff does not attend the hearing, the court will end the hearing, except when the defendant shows interest in the continuation of proceedings. If the defendant does not appear before the court, the hearing will be celebrated with the plaintiff.

The hearing will begin with the allegation of the plaintiff and after that the defendant can allege whatever he thinks is necessary to defend his rights, including the opposition of procedural exceptions. Following that, evidence will be introduced, if necessary, and finally the judgment will be issued within a ten-day period.

C. The Judgment

101. The judgment is subject to the form that is stated in Article 209 NCCP:

- Name of the court, name of the judge or judges, date, names of the parties, attorneys and representatives.
- Claims that have been introduced, alleged facts, evidence and facts which the judge consider as proved facts. (All this data is called and it is written under the name 'Antecedentes de Hecho').
- Under the so-called Fundamentos de Derecho, the judge will offer the reasons in law and, finally, he comes to the decision or 'Fallo'. If the judgment is issued by several judges, it has to be passed by a majority vote, but dissenting opinions can

be written separately. After the judgment is issued, the court cannot alter it but it is possible to clarify any concept and to modify material errors. (Article 214 NCCP and Article 267 LOPJ).

102. There are different kinds of judgments: On the merits (deciding the case between the parties), judgments before stating the law (deciding on a procedural exception) and provisional (deciding the case but these judgments are not res judicata and it is possible, under certain conditions, to initiate new proceedings).

103. Article 222 NCCP states that when a judgment has been issued and reviewed, it is not possible for a new process with the same object to be allowed. It is res judicata. Res judicata covers the facts that have been decided in the judgment and the prayers for relief of the claim and counterclaim. The parties and their successors are bound by it. Judgments rendered in matters such as civil status, matrimonial proceedings, paternity, maternity and capacity oblige everybody, not only the parties, if they are inscribed in a public record.

Res judicata has another effect which is called positive function. According to Article 222.4 NCCP the judgment issued by a judge obliges another court in a posterior proceeding when in the latter the parties are the same and the judgment already rendered is a logical precedent of the case that has to be tried.

It must be underlined that the NCCP abandons the theory of res judicata as presumption of truth as was defined in Article 1252 of the CC.

When a judgment is res judicata it can be enforced without question.

104. The judge completes his duty when the judgment is issued, but the parties can ask the judge to clarify or to interpret the judgment (Articles 267 LOPJ and 214 NCCP). Article 215 NCCP establishes a proceeding to be followed in case a judgment is not complete because the judge forgot to answer any of the questions addressed by a party. Finally, Article 240 LOPJ and Article 228 NCCP state that the parties can ask the judge to annul the proceedings if the judgment has been issued in violation of essential procedural norms which have violated the fundamental right of defence in the proceedings.

105. Provisional enforcement is also permitted by the law under the circumstances prescribed in Articles 524–537 NCCP.

II. Provisional Proceedings

A. *Default Proceedings*

106. According to Article 496 NCCP when the defendant, summoned in a legal form, does not appear before the Court on a specified date or in a period of time he shall be declared in default. This is not generally considered as admission, except otherwise stated by the law.

The decision declaring the defendant in default will be notified by mail if the domicile is known. If the domicile is unknown, the notification will be carried out by the publication of a notice in the public board of the Court or in public or private newspapers. The judgment will be notified personally to the defendant if possible. Otherwise, it shall be published in public bulletins.

107. The law considers that a judgment in default has been issued through adversarial proceedings. This presumption means that the judgment can only be objected according to the cases stated in Article 501 NCCP:

- The defendant could not appear before the Court due to circumstances beyond his control as *vis major*.
- The defendant was totally unaware of the claim because the writ of summons was not served to him in his domicile.
- The defendant has been summoned by public notice and has been absent from the place where the trial was carried out.

108. The opposition to the judgment in default has to be lodged according to the time limit stated in Article 502 NCCP and if the defendant gets a favourable decision, the prior judgment is annulled and the case is retried through a special proceeding.

Chapter 3. Review Proceedings

109. Three types of review proceedings are distinguished under Spanish law: Ordinary review proceedings ('reposición', 'queja' and appeal), extraordinary review (cassation and review by infringement of procedural norms) and exceptional review proceedings to annul the res judicata of a judgment.

110. 'Reposición' (Articles 451–454 NCCP) is based on procedural infringements, which occurred at any time during the proceeding, and is decided by the same court that has the competence in that proceeding. It is possible, likewise, to appeal for reversal of certain decisions of the clerk.

111. 'Queja' (Articles 494–495 NCCP) is based on the possibility of no admission of appeal or cassation and it is the competence of the Superior Court that declares the inadmissibility of appeal, cassation or review based on procedural infringements.

§1. Appeal

I. Conditions to Appeal

112. As mentioned above (paragraph 14), Spanish law is based on the principle of the double layer of jurisdiction except in oral proceedings of EUR 3,000 or less. According to Article 455 NCCP, the judgments, in all types of proceedings, can be appealed. Some interlocutory orders that bring the case to an end can also be appealed. It is important to understand that, in a technical way, the second instance is only open when the judgment on the merits has been appealed.

113. The judgments of the Justice of the Peace can be appealed to the judges of first instance (in this particular case acting as judges of second instance). The judgments of the judges of first instance can be appealed to the Provincial Courts. In fact, following the amendment of NCCP in October 2011, the sentences handed down by Judges of the Peace are not appealable, because they only have competence in very small amount cases.

The Provincial Courts are also competent to resolve appeals against judgments of the Commercial Courts and, where appropriate, of those issued by the Judges of Violence against Women.

II. Appeal Proceedings

114. It is possible to distinguish several stages in appeal proceedings.

A. Filing of the Appeal

115. The appeal has to be filed within a twenty-day term from the date the judgment is notified to the party. A written document has to be presented exposing the reasons upon which the appeal is based. The reasons can basically be of two types.

116. Appeal based on procedural infringements during first instance proceedings with reference to the precise norm that has been infringed. If the infringement of the law occurred during the proceedings (the infringement of a procedural norm is also possible in the judgment), the law requires objection as soon as possible. The appellant can ask the court to annul the proceedings as a whole or in part. If the court rules in favour of the appellant, the court will order a retrial of the case from the very moment the infringement occurred. If the violation of the procedural law has occurred in the final judgment of first instance the Court of Appeal will issue a new judgment in place of the one that has been reversed.

117. Appeal based on the infringement of substantive law. The appeal can be based on two types of errors:

(1) errors of the judge of first instance solving the points of law in dispute or
(2) mistakes caused by the court resolving the questions that have arisen about the facts.

The appellant asks that the first instance judgment is revoked and the Provincial Court will issue a new judgment.

118. The other party will be notified of the appeal and he shall have ten days to present a written document opposing the appellant or even appealing the judgment himself. If the latter is the case, the first appellant has to be informed of the new appeal and he has ten days to say whatever he thinks is necessary to protect his rights.

119. The proceedings that we have described above are before the judge of first instance. When the proceedings are finished, the case is sent to the Provincial Court or to the judge of first instance if the Judges of the Peace issued the judgment appealed.

120. Proceedings before the Provincial Court can be of two types.

121. First, proceedings without a hearing, when evidence is not necessary or inadmissible. In this case, the Court of Appeal has to issue the new judgment in thirty days.

Second, the clerk of the appeals court will set a date for a trial when evidence has to be introduced. After the trial, the court must give its opinion within ten days.

III. Scope of Appeal

122. The type of appeal that Spanish law allows is a limited appeal. Limited appeal has the following characteristics:

(1) If the appellant is the plaintiff, it is not possible to either introduce new actions or change the facts upon which the action is based.
(2) If the appellant is the defendant, it is not possible to change the causes upon which the opposition is based.
(3) It is possible to introduce new pleadings but without altering the object of the proceedings.
(4) Evidence during appeal is also limited to the following cases, according to Article 460 NCCP:
  - Evidence that the first instance judge wrongly did not admit.
  - Evidence that was admitted in first instance, but was impossible to introduce.
  - Evidence about relevant facts that occurred after the first instance judgment or evidence about facts that were unknown during first instance proceedings.

§2. Extraordinary Review Based on the Infringement of Procedural Law

123. One of the main changes in the NCCP is the division of the old cassation in two different types of review: The new extraordinary review based on the infringement of procedural law and cassation. Nevertheless, it is important to take into account that this new system is not in force yet because the LOPJ must first be modified. The Government had enough votes in Congress to pass the NCCP, but it could not modify the LOPJ because Article 81 of the Constitution requires a majority vote of one-half plus one to pass or to modify the so-called organic laws. Until the new regulation is approved, this extraordinary review shall be the competence of the TS and the judgments that can be appealed will be those for which cassation is possible, according to final disposition sixteen of the NCCP.

124. The civil division of the Superior Court of Justice of the Autonomous Regions can review judgments of second instance, according to Article 468 NCCP.

125. This extraordinary appeal can only be based on the following causes (Article 469 NCCP):

- Infringement of the norms of jurisdiction and competence.
- Infringement of the norms with which final judgments have to comply.
- Infringement of procedural norms or infringement of the essential guaranties of process.
- Infringements of the constitutional rights of Article 24 CE.

126. According to Article 476 NCCP the judgment will be null if the case is reversed based on case (i). In all other cases, the judgment will be null and proceedings have to continue from the very moment that the infringement of procedural law took place.

§3. CASSATION

I. General Characteristics

127. The TS is competent to decide cassation, except in particular cases based on the substantive law of the Autonomous Communities. If the latter is the case, the Superior Court of the Autonomous Community will be the competent one.

128. According to Article 477 NCCP, cassation has as its only objective to control the infringement of substantive law in judgments of second instance in the following cases:

(1) When the judgment has violated constitutional rights, except for those stated in Article 24 of the Constitution.
(2) When the value of the claim is more than EUR 600,000.
(3) When it involves what the law calls ‘cassational interest’. This is a new concept which has been introduced by the NCCP. A case is considered to have ‘cassational interest’ when:
    (a) The judgment which is appealed is contrary to the jurisprudence of the TS.
    (b) The judgment which is appealed is contradictory with other judgments rendered by other Provincial Courts.
    (c) The judgment which is appealed is based on a law that has been passed less than five years ago, except when there is already jurisprudence of the TS.

For the correct application of the NCCP in this matter, it is very important to study the so-called Acuerdo of the Civil Chamber of the TS of 27 January 2017.

129. It is important to underline that cassation is not a new instance in the sense that it is not possible to challenge the facts of the judgment. The TS only has to determine if the Provincial Court has properly applied the substantive law (i.e., the proper law has been chosen and correctly construed). As we have said above, the word ‘law’ refers to substantive law, including constitutional rights (except Article 24 CE) and Law of the European Communities and Treaties which have been signed by Spain.

II. Cassation Proceedings

We have to distinguish the following stages in cassation proceedings.

A. Filing (Articles 479–482 NCCP)

130. The first stage of cassation proceedings takes place before the Provincial Court in which the judgment was rendered.

The written document of filing has to be lodged within twenty days, according to the different cases stated in Article 479. In the document, the party has to reason the motives upon which cassation is based.

B. Declaration of Admissibility

131. Once the written document which explains the motives is filed, proceedings before the Provincial Court are finished and the case is sent to the TS (or sometimes, as mentioned above in paragraph 124, to the Superior Court of the Autonomous Communities). Cassation can be inadmissible if:

- Legal requirements are not fulfilled.
- The value of the case is less than EUR 600,000.
- The case has no cassational interest.
- Cassation will also be inadmissible when it is manifestly unfounded or similar cases have been previously dismissed.

If cassation is admissible, the other party can oppose at this moment.

C. Decision

132. In some cases, a hearing is possible before the decision. Otherwise, the TS will decide the case without a hearing.

The judgment of the TS can quash a judgment. Partial quashing is possible. The TS does not remit the case to a lower Court but it decides the case in all circumstances. Remitting the case was possible when the TS dealt with procedural infringements but it is not possible under the NCCP. Nevertheless, until the LOPJ is revised the TS deals with cassation and extraordinary review based on infringement of procedural law at the same time.

§4. Extraordinary Appeals

I. Petition for Review (*Recurso de Revisión*)

133. Petitions for review are only possible in the cases exhaustively stated in Article 510 NCCP:

(a) If after the judgment, conclusive documents appear or documents concealed by a party are retrieved.

(b) If the judgment was based on false documents or they have been declared false in criminal proceedings that took place after the judgment.
(c) If the judgment was based on witnesses or expert witnesses whose depositions or reports have been declared false in criminal proceedings that took place after the judgment.
(d) If the judgment was issued based on violence, deception or bribery.
(e) The Organic Law 7/2015 of July 21 has added a new case. It is also possible when the European Court of Human Rights declares that the sentence was handed down in violation of the rights recognized in the Convention and its Protocols, provided that the violation persists and cannot cease in any other way than through the review. This review cannot harm the rights acquired in good faith by third parties.
(f) It is necessary that the judgment is final. If other review proceedings are possible they must be used.

134. The competent court is the TS or, in some cases, the Superior Court of the Autonomous Communities.

135. The petition for review has to be filed within five years subsequent to the final judgment and within three months after the motive has been discovered.

The TS, prior to examining the case, will summon all the parties involved and once the parties have appeared before the Court 'oral proceedings' will follow. In all cases, the Public Attorney must be informed.

136. A petition of this type does not have a suspensive effect, but the enforcement of the judgment can be suspended if the petitioner offers a bond to cover any possible damages. The parties and the Public Attorney have to be heard, for this purpose.

137. If there is cause for review and this cause has been crucial in the judgment, the TS quashes the judgment and the case has to be retried by the competent court.

138. The Organic Law 1/2009 of November 3, which amends LOPJ, establishes that in order to lodge an appeal in civil jurisdiction it is necessary to set up a deposit. (The amount is different depending on the type of review proceedings). If the appeal is won, in whole or in part, the amount will be refunded. Otherwise, these amounts will be dedicated to finance free legal aid and modernize the administration of justice.

Part V. Incidents

139. Normally, when the plaintiff introduces an action, the subsequent proceedings continue in due course until a judgment is rendered. But the proceedings can be disturbed by causes of different nature, both external and internal, giving rise to an 'incident'. We are going to enunciate the main incidents. In this concept of incidents, we include the possibility that a criminal problem arises in the course of civil proceedings.

§1. Criminal Problems in the Course of Civil Proceedings

140. If in the course of a civil proceeding a fact arises that can be considered a crime, the court will inform the Public Attorney and he or she shall decide if criminal proceedings are necessary. In that case, civil proceedings will be suspended when the following requisites are fulfilled:

- Criminal proceedings have begun.
- The decision of the criminal court is decisive for the resolution of the civil case.

141. Civil proceedings will be suspended with an order of the court, at the end of the proceedings, just before the judgment is rendered. (Article 40 NCCP)

§2. Joinder of Actions

142. Joinder of actions is possible in the following cases, according to Articles 76 and 98 NCCP:

- When the judgment of one of the proceedings could be 'prejudicial' for the other case.
- When actions are related and if they are decided in separate judgments contradictory decisions are possible.
- In cases of bankruptcy or proceedings in succession cases.

143. Joinder of actions is only possible when a party asks for it because the judge cannot order it ex officio. The actions can be in different proceedings before different courts. Conditions and requisites are stated in Articles 86–98 of the NCCP.

§3. CHALLENGE OF JUDGES

144. Challenge of judges is foreseen both in LOPJ and in NCCP. It has to be based on one of the causes stated in Article 219 LOPJ which we can resume as follows:

- Being a relative of the parties, their representatives or lawyers.
- Interest in the decision.
- Lack of impartiality.

Proceedings in cases that challenge a judge are in Articles 221–228 LOPJ and Articles 101–119 NCCP.

§4. TERMINATION OF AN ACTION

145. Proceedings normally end with a judgment, but there are other ways to terminate a case, each one of them with different consequences.

I. Time Limitation (*caducidad de la instancia*)

146. A suit that has been filed elapses if there is no activity by the parties for two years from the time the proceedings are in first instance or after one year if review proceedings are being followed (Article 237 NCCP). Time limitation is declared ex officio by the judge. If time limitation is declared in first instance there is no res judicata. If time limitation is declared during appeal, cassation or extraordinary review based on the infringement of procedural norms, the judgment that has been 'appealed' is final and it may be res judicata.

II. Suspension

147. Suspension of proceedings is allowed for a sixty-day period as stated in Article 19.4 NCCP.

III. Discontinuance of a Claim

148. According to Article 20.2 NCCP the plaintiff can discontinue a claim at any time, but if the defendant has already appeared before the judge he has the right to be heard prior to the judge's decision. If the defendant agrees, then the judge will issue an order that ends the proceedings. The basic rule in this case is that the plaintiff has to pay the defendant for any costs incurred.

IV. Abandonment of the Action

149. Article 20.1 NCCP allows the plaintiff to abandon the action. In this case a judgment will be issued and the defendant will be acquitted. The plaintiff has to pay the defendant for any costs incurred.

V. Agreement to the Claim

150. Agreement to the claim means that the defendant recognizes that the claim is well founded. (Article 21 NCCP). Agreement is not permitted when it is contrary to the public interest, against the law or prejudicial for a third party.

Agreement to a judgment means that the party renounces to review proceedings.

VI. Settlement

151. Settlements during proceedings are allowed at any moment and it is possible to say that they are encouraged. If a settlement is reached, it has to be approved by the judge and it is enforceable as a judgment.

152. Finally, if during the course of the proceedings legitimate interests disappear, the proceedings can end (Article 22 NCCP).

Part VI. Legal Cost and Legal Aid

Chapter 1. Legal Costs

153. Part VI, Ch. 1., Legal Costs. It is obvious that there are considerable expenses in the administration of justice. But of all those expenses we can distinguish several types:

(a) Costs of maintenance of the court system, which includes payment of the judges and other public servants. In Spain the Central Government or the Government of the Autonomous Communities pays all those expenses.
(b) Costs in the course of a particular proceeding. Two types of costs can be distinguished:
  (i) Those in direct relation with the proceedings.
  (ii) Those that do not have a direct relation with the proceedings.

154. Article 241 NCCP determines what expenses can be considered costs as stated in (b)[i]:

- Lawyers' and representatives' fees when their intervention is required.
- Public notices that have to be published during proceedings.
- Bonds.
- Expert witness fees.
- Certified copies of documents.
- Other expenses that are required using a scale.
- Taxes that have to be paid in certain cases.

155. Article 394 NCCP states that legal costs have to be paid by the losing party except when the judge, in a reasoned decision, affirms that the case was especially difficult either in the determination of facts or in resolving points of law. That, of course, means that the prevailing party has a right to be reimbursed by the losing party. In case of partial relief, each party will pay its own costs. The losing party can impugn the costs either because he or she thinks that there are items that cannot be included or because he or she thinks that they are excessive.

Chapter 2. Legal Aid

156. Article 119 CE reads that the administration of justice will be free for those without economic resources. Legal aid was reformed by Law 1/96 of Free Legal Assistance (Ley de Asistancia Jurídica Gratuita); this law was completed by Decree 2103/96, later replaced by RD 996/2003.

157. Legal aid is available to the following people and legal persons:

- Spanish citizens and citizens of other countries of the European Union.
- Foreigners who are legal residents in Spain. In criminal cases and cases of asylum, legal aid is also available for illegal residents in Spain.
- Social security institutions.
- Associations of public interest.
- Foundations.
- Employees in labour courts.

158. Legal aid can be total or partial, depending on the income of the petitioner. In order to grant free legal assistance, the Public Income Indicator of Multiple Effects (*'Indicador Público de Renta de Efectos Múltiples', IPREM)* will be taken into account. This benchmark is used as a reference in Spain for the allocation of grants, subsidies or unemployment benefits, among others.

159. Legal aid is available in all types of courts and proceedings either as claimant or as defendant. The Provincial Commission of Free Legal Aid (Article 10 LAJG) grants the aid. Members of the legal profession and the Public Administration integrate the Commission but there are no judges. If the Commission does not grant free legal aid, the decision can be appealed to a judge.

Each bar must organize a list of members who provide legal aid when it is granted (Articles 22–36 of LAJG deals with the proceedings). The Ministry of Justice (or the competent body of the Autonomous Community) through the bar pays these lawyers and representatives, taking into account the type of proceedings.

Part VII. Evidence

Chapter 1. Burden of Proof

160. Article 217 NCCP establishes the rules of burden of proof. These rules mainly refer to facts, but facts are not necessarily the only object of proof. Foreign laws applicable to a particular case must be proven, but the court can apply them using its own means of investigation. Customs (costumbre) must also be proved except when the parties agree on its existence. A fact introduced by a party does not necessarily have to be proven if the other party admits that the fact is true, except in cases such as divorce, capacity, legal status (Article 281.2 NCCP). Facts that are generally known do not have to be proven (Article 281.3 NCCP).

161. Article 217.2 NCCP states that the plaintiff must prove the fact in which his right is founded. The defendant has to prove the facts brought forward and on which his defence is based.

Finally, Article 217.6 NCCP says that these rules have to be construed taking into account which facts are more accessible to the parties.

There are special rules in certain proceedings, for example, those which refer to unfair competition, misleading advertising or sex discrimination.

Chapter 2. Admissibility of Evidence

162. Article 299 NCCP states the means that a party can use to prove facts in a civil proceeding:

- Deposition by the parties.
- Public documents (usually those drawn up by a notary public).
- Private documents.
- Expert witnesses.
- Inspection by the judge him- or herself.
- Deposition by witnesses.
- Means of reproduction of sounds and images and computer data.
- Whatever means that may be useful to prove a fact.

163. Although presumptions are not a means of proof, judges can use them to establish a fact as true. There are two kinds of presumptions: Those that have been established by the law (Article 385 NCCP) and those that the judge establishes by him- or herself (Article 386 NCCP). In both cases, it is necessary that the fact, on which the presumption is based, is proven.

164. Article 11 LOPJ and Article 287 NCCP prescribe that evidence is illegal and null if obtained in violation of constitutional rights.

165. Sometimes, there are rules that the judge has to follow to establish a fact as true. We refer to these rules as 'legal proof'. There are some rules of this type in Spanish law:

- In public documents: Articles 319–323 NCCP and Articles 1218–1221 of the CC.
- In private documents: Articles 1225–1230 of the CC and Article 326 NCCP.
- In deposition by the parties: Article 316 NCCP.

166. In other cases, judges are not bound by law and they have to reach the truth through 'intimate conviction' or 'moral proof'.

167. Article 120 CE and Article 218.2 NCCP state that the judge has to motivate the factual components of the judgment. For that purpose, they have to use the rules of legal proof and they must show the logical reasoning used to set a fact as true.

168. Each party has to propose the evidence that they want to use in the proceedings (Article 281.1 NCCP). The judge has to decide what evidence is admissible (Article 285 NCCP).

Chapter 3. Administration of Evidence

§1. Forced Production of Documents

169. The general rule stated in Article 265 NCCP is that private and public documents have to be introduced with the claim and the defence. Both public and private documents have to be presented in its original form, but copies are allowed if they comply with the circumstances stated in Articles 267 and 268 NCCP. The authenticity of the copies can be challenged. Documents can also be presented at a later time in cases prescribed in Article 270:

- Documents of a later date.
- Unknown documents when the claim or the defence was presented.
- Inaccessible documents when the claim or the defence was presented.

No document can be introduced after the trial.

170. The parties usually produce documents in a voluntary way. One party has to provide the other party with a copy of each document introduced in the proceedings.

Article 328 NCCP prescribes that each party can ask the other to exhibit a document. If the party refuses to exhibit it, the judge can presume from such conduct that the simple copy of the document presented is authentic (Article 329 NCCP). The judge can also order the party to produce the document if the judge thinks that the document is necessary and relevant.

According to Article 330 NCCP, the judge can order a third party to exhibit a document. The Public Administration has to exhibit all the documents under its custody and certified copies have to be issued when requested by a court unless otherwise stated by law to preserve legal secrets (Article 332 NCCP).

171. A party can challenge the authenticity of a private document. If it is a handwritten document the party can say that it is not his, but normally the documents are typed and in this case the party can affirm that it is not his signature. The authenticity of the document can be verified through a special proceeding which is called 'cotejo de letras' and is conducted by an expert in graphology, under the supervision of a judge. The proceeding consists of comparing the handwritten document or the signature with an authentic document. If there is no document to be compared, the judge will dictate a text to serve as an authentic document.

172. A public document is authentic by itself but a party can argue that it is a forgery. Forgery is a crime punishable with a maximum of six years of imprisonment. In this case the civil proceedings will be suspended, and the crime will be prosecuted (Article 40 NCCP).

§2. Deposition by Witnesses

173. A witness is a person who gives evidence in a cause before a court and he testifies about facts that he knows and that are relevant to the cause.

174. Everybody can be a witness, even a minor, if the judge, considering their mental maturity, allows them. People of diminished mental capacity are excluded (Article 361 NCCP).

I. Duties and Rights of a Witness

A. *Duties*

175. The first duty is appearing before the court when the witness has been summoned in a legal form. The infringement of this duty is punishable with a fine of up to EUR 600. If the witness does not finally appear, he shall be prosecuted for contempt of court (Article 292 NCCP).

The witness has to testify under oath or affirmation (Article 365 NCCP), except when he is a minor. He or she shall be advised of the crimes regarding perjury (Article 458 CP).

The witness has to answer every question and he or she has to answer truthfully.

B. *Rights*

176. The witness has the right to be compensated for the expenses incurred (Article 375 NCCP).

II. Deposition Proceedings

177. Deposition by witnesses takes place in an oral hearing. First, the Court will inquire if the witness has any relation with the case, in order to establish whether the testimony will be impartial (Article 367 NCCP).

A party can challenge the impartiality of a witness according to Article 377 NCCP.

The party that has presented the witness will begin the interrogatory. If a question is not relevant the judge will declare it inadmissible. The other party can also object if he thinks that the question is not relevant or if the question includes something other than a fact. After the first interrogatory, there is cross-examination.

The judge can also question the witness (Article 372.2 NCCP).

178. The hearing will be videotaped and the registrar of the Court will keep the tapes (Article 147 NCCP).

179. Affidavits are also allowed for legal persons, Article 381 NCCP.

§3. Deposition by the Parties Themselves

180. Each party can examine the other party about relevant facts to the case. The deposition by the parties will take place in a hearing, in an oral form. The questions have to be admitted by the judge (Article 302 NCCP).

If a party does not appear before the court to be interrogated by the other party, the judge may consider this conduct as recognition of facts when these facts are prejudicial for the party (Article 304 NCCP).

The court can ask the parties questions to clarify the facts (Article 306 NCCP). When the party refuses to answer a question, the judge may interpret his silence as recognition of prejudicial facts (Article 307 NCCP).

If the party has recognized as true a fact in which it has personally intervened and which is prejudicial for it, the judge is bound to that declaration (Article 316 NCCP).

§4. Expert Evidence

181. Article 335 NCCP states that expert witnesses are admissible when scientific, artistic or technical knowledge is required to solve a problem of fact. Though the expert's job is to clarify a case with his technical expertise, the judge is not bound by the expert opinion. The law requires a university degree to intervene as an expert in the proceedings (Article 340 NCCP), but sometimes these rules have exceptions such as the cases stated in Articles 142 (interpreters) or 638 NCCP (to appraise the value of property). Besides being an expert, the law requires that he or she must be impartial. For this reason, expert witnesses can be challenged according to Articles 343–344 NCCP.

182. The expert evidence can be introduced in the proceedings in two ways:

(1) Expert reports presented with the claim and defence (Article 336 NCCP). If those reports are not available at a particular moment, the party can introduce this evidence at a later moment, but always before the first hearing of the proceedings. Once the report has been introduced, the parties have to say if they want the expert witness to be summoned to appear in the trial (Article 337 NCCP).

(2) In cases of legal aid or when a party requests it, an expert designated by the court can introduce the expert evidence. The expert witness will be drawn among names included in a list of experts that every year will be made by cultural and scientific institutions. In this case, the expert has to accept the case and he can request compensation, if needed, because as a professional he has the right to collect fees (Article 342 NCCP). Expert advice is generally very expensive. After the report is made, the expert witness may be summoned to the trial to answer the questions asked by the judge and the parties in an adversarial proceeding.

§5. Inspection by Judge

183. The judge can inspect places, objects and persons by himself (Article 353 NCCP).

The inspection is made by the judge, but the parties can intervene to respect the adversary principle.

When a place or object has to be inspected, the judge can order whatever is necessary, including the entrance to any premises (Article 354 NCCP).

The inspection of a person will take place by interrogating him (Article 355 NCCP) and the dignity and intimacy of the person inspected have to be respected (Article 355.2 NCCP).

During the inspection, the judge can hear the parties and testimony of witnesses and expert evidence can be required (Articles 356–357 NCCP). It is possible to videotape or record the act of inspection (Article 359 NCCP). In all cases, the registrar will draw a document with all the particulars of the case (Article 359 NCCP).

§6. Means of Reproduction of Sound, Image or Computer Data

184. The parties can introduce as evidence videotapes, tapes, etc. When this evidence is presented, the party has to enclose a written transcription. The authenticity of this material can be challenged (Article 382 NCCP). In the same way, the parties can introduce computer data. The authenticity of this data can also be challenged (Article 384 NCCP).

Part VIII. Particular Proceedings

185. In the NCCP (Book IV), the so-called special proceedings are regulated, divided into three different titles. In Title I, the law refers to proceedings in legal capacity, paternity, maternity, separation and divorce and minority of age. In Title II, the NCCP deals with the judicial division of a patrimony, and in Title III, the NCCP establishes special proceedings to protect a credit.

§1. Proceedings in Matters of Legal Capacity, Maternity, Paternity, Separation and Divorce and Minors of Age

186. All these proceedings have several notes in common:

- The proceedings are less adversarial in the sense that the judge has more power than in ordinary proceedings, and he can intervene in a more active way to prove the relevant facts (Article 752 NCCP).
- In most of the cases, the intervention of the Public Attorney is required (Article 749 NCCP).
- The parties cannot give up their rights and in some cases it is necessary that the Public Attorney agrees (Article 751 NCCP).
- In these proceedings, the hearings may be closed to the public (Article 753 NCCP).
- The proceedings to follow are the so-called oral proceedings and the defence is written (Article 753 NCCP).

187. We are not going to explain each of the proceedings mentioned in Title I of Book IV, but a few notes of proceedings in matters of separation and divorce will be explained, because they are very often used.

I. Separation and Divorce Proceedings

A. *Venue*

188. The competent judge is one of the domicile of the parties. If the parties live in different districts, the competent judge will be chosen by the plaintiff from the judges of the last common domicile or from the place where the defendant lives

(Article 769.1 NCCP). There are special rules in cases regarding people without domicile and in cases where the domicile is unknown.

B. Proceedings

189. There are two kinds of proceedings: (1) Those without mutual consent and (2) those with mutual consent (Articles 770 and 777 NCCP). It is not possible to describe all the particulars of marriage proceedings with all the related questions regarding, for example rights in property arising out of a matrimonial relationship, custody of children.

190. Proceedings without mutual consent. (Articles 770–776 NCCP). As mentioned above, oral proceedings have to be followed, but with a few particularities:

- Documents that have to be presented with the claim (Article 770.1 NCCP):
  - Certified copy of marriage.
  - Birth certificates of the children (if there are any).
  - Documents that show the financial situation, for example tax forms, payrolls, property titles.
- Counterclaim is only permitted if it is related with the matrimonial proceedings (Article 770.2 NCCP).
- If the parties agree, the proceedings can be changed to mutual consent proceedings.
- Prior to the presentation of the claim, the future plaintiff can ask the judge to rule over provisional measures, such as child custody, visitation rights, use of property of the marriage These measures will be taken after a hearing and the claim has to be introduced within thirty days. These measures can also be requested at the same time the claim is introduced.
- A separation agreement (convenio regulador) can be presented by the parties, which can provide the payment of alimony, division of property and support of the children. This agreement can be modified if the circumstances change (Articles 774–775 NCCP). This agreement is enforceable and the party that does not comply can be fined (Article 776 NCCP) and can even be prosecuted (Article 227 Penal Code (Código Penal (CP))).

191. Proceedings with mutual consent (Article 777 NCCP). These proceedings are characterized by the fact that a hearing is not always required. The petition must be presented by both spouses with the same documents mentioned above and a separation agreement also is required. If there are minors, the Public Attorney must be heard. The judge can approve separation or divorce, but he can reject the separation agreement and in that case he shall give the spouse a ten-day term to present a new agreement (very often the separation agreement is rejected because the judge thinks that it is not good enough for the children or it is too favourable for one of the parties).

Article 87 of the CC has been amended to allow divorce with mutual consent without the intervention of a judge. It is necessary to present a petition, with a separation agreement, before a public notary or the clerk of the court.

§2. Division of Property

192. Book IV, Title II of the NCCP, deals with judicial division of property and it distinguishes two kinds of division: (1) Division of wills and succession (Articles 782–805 NCCP) and (2) division of matrimonial property (Articles 806–811 NCCP).

§3. Proceedings to Protect a Credit

193. Book IV, Title III of the NCCP, establishes two types of proceedings to obtain an enforceable decision very quickly: The so-called proceso monitorio and the so-called proceso cambiario.

The first one is intended for claims of any amount based on private documents, even when they are not signed by the debtor (Article 812 NCCP). When the claim is introduced (a form can be used) the debtor will be required to pay or to oppose it (Articles 814–815 NCCP). If the debtor does not appear before the Court, an enforceable order will be issued. If the debtor appears before the Court and he challenges the claim, proceedings based on the value of the claim have to begin (Article 818 NCCP).

The second proceeding is based on documents such as checks, promissory notes and bills of exchange (Article 819 NCCP). The proceedings begin with a succinct claim. The judge will examine the claim and if it is correct, he or she shall issue an order requiring the debtor to pay and he or she shall also issue a preventive garnishee order (Article 821 NCCP). The debtor can oppose only by the causes stated in Article 67 of the Law that rules checks and bills of exchange. (Article 824 NCCP). If the debtor does not oppose, the order will be enforceable (Article 825).

If the debtor opposes the claim, the parties will be summoned to a hearing (Article 827). The judgment is not res judicata to a full extension (Article 827 NCCP).

Obviously, in Spain Regulation 1896/06 of the Parliament and European Council applies.

§4. Non-Contentious Matter

194. The NCCP does not deal with non-contentious matter and Book III LEC of 1881 was still in force. Finally, Law 2/2015, of July 2, was approved and has replaced the old regulation. Article 1 of the Law defines non-contentious matter as a matter in which the judge has to intervene, or the intervention is necessary, in the absence of a dispute. There is a large number of situations in which the judge is requested to intervene, in civil and commercial matters.

The new law divides the different voluntary jurisdiction procedures into the following titles:

- Persons: Refers specifically to matters relating to minors, persons with disabilities or with lack of capacity, declaration of absence or death, organ transplants from live donors (Articles 23–80 LJV).
- Family: Matters relating to parental custody or marriage: Articles 81-90 LJV.
- Wills and testaments: Articles 91-95 LJV.
- Obligations and contracts: Articles 96-99 LJV.
- Property and real rights: Articles 100-107 LJV.
- Voluntary auctions: Articles 108-111 LJV.
- Commercial matters, specifically various issues related to societies: Articles 112-137 LJV.
- Conciliation: Articles 139-148 LJV.

195. It is impossible to explain in detail all those proceedings, but there are general rules that apply to all of them (Articles 1-22 Law 2/2.15)):

- They are not parties in the strict sense.
- The proceedings may be initiated by the judge, Public Attorney or interested party. The request must follow the form established in Article 14 of the Law. Interested parties will be summoned to a hearing and, eventually evidence may be introduced. Finally, the judge or the Secretario Judicial will decide.
- The Public Attorney has to be heard in matters related with minors or where the public interest can be affected (Article 4 LJV).
- The decision of the judge can be appealed (Article 20.2 LJV).
- The intervention of lawyers and representatives of the parties (procuradores) is not always required (Article 3.2 LJV)
- People who have an interest in the case can be heard (Article 3.1 LJV)
- It is not possible to begin or continue a voluntary jurisdiction case when there is a contentious proceeding, on the same matter, already in progress (Article 6.2 LJV).
- The decision of a voluntary jurisdiction case does not prevent the initiation of a subsequent contentious process in which the judge can rule upon the decision previously adopted (Article 19.4 LJV).

Part IX. Enforcement of Judgments and Seizure for Security

Chapter 1. Enforcement of Judgments

§1. Enforcement of Domestic Judgments

196. The NCCP deals with the enforcement of judgments in Book III (Articles 517–720). This is one of the subjects that the new law has changed with respect to the old one. Under Spanish law (Article 117.3 CE and Article 2 LOPJ) jurisdiction means not only to judge but also to enforce the judgment. For that reason, enforcement of judgments is also full competence of the court system acting through decisions and acts of coercion, if necessary. Obviously, in the latter case the courts are helped by other public servants, even by the police. The right to enforce the judgment is considered a constitutional right based on Article 24 CE as the TC has ruled in numerous cases.

The competent court to enforce a judgment is the court that dealt with proceedings in which the judgment was rendered in first instance (Article 545.1 NCCP).

In the proceedings to enforce judgments there are also two parties: (1) The creditor (ejecutante) and (2) the debtor (ejecutado).

The main characteristics of proceedings for the enforcement of a judgment will be explained in a very simplified way.

I. Beginning of Enforcement Proceedings

197. The proceedings will begin with a claim to enforce the judgment ('demanda ejecutiva'). Article 549 NCCP states the requisites of this claim in which intervention of lawyers and 'procuradores' are required:

- Competent court.
- Identification of the parties.
- Judgment which has to be enforced.
- Relief that it is sought.
- Property of the debtor which the creditor can identify.
- Measures to be taken to find the property of the debtor.

The claim has to be presented with all the documents mentioned in Article 550 NCCP.

198. The judge has to examine if the claim is presented in a legal form. If so, the court will issue an order. This order can have one of the following decisions: (a) if the judges refuse to enforce the judgment, the creditor can appeal, or (b) if the order allows the enforcement, the order cannot be appealed but the debtor can oppose to it later (Articles 551–552 NCCP).

199. The debtor can oppose the order within ten days from the moment the decision was served. He can allege that he has complied with the decision as a basic way of opposition. The debtor can also oppose the order based on procedural exceptions.

200. The NCCP distinguishes two different types of enforcement proceedings:

- Enforcement of judgments ordering the debtor to pay a sum of money (which in Spanish is called 'ejecución genérica').
- Other cases (which is called 'ejecución específica').

II. Enforcement of Judgments Ordering the Debtor to Pay a Sum of Money

201. If the debtor does not pay the sum of money he owes, measures of enforcement will be taken. The property of the debtor will be sold to pay the creditor or, if the property consists of money, it will be given to the creditor. The first thing to do is to find the property of the debtor and seize it.

The property that can be seized is stated in Article 592 NCCP:

- Money or bank accounts.
- Credits, shares, bonds, etc.
- Jewellery or art objects.
- Income, profits, rents, etc.
- Interests, natural and civil fruits of property.
- Chattel.
- Immovable property.
- Earnings (with the limits of Article 607 NCCP).
- A company as a whole.

202. There are several measures to guarantee the property that has been seized, as stated in Articles 621–623 NCCP, depending on the type of property that has been seized.

203. The NCCP foresees several ways of paying the creditor:

- Direct pay of money, banks accounts, foreign money, etc. The sum of money which is owed will be given to the creditor. No special proceedings are required for this purpose (Article 634 NCCP).
- If the property that has been seized consists of shares, these will be sold in the stock exchange to pay the creditor (Article 635 NCCP).
- The NCCP allows that the creditor and debtor agree on the way that the credit will be paid (Article 636 NCCP).
- The NCCP has introduced the possibility of selling the property by a specialized person or company (Articles 636 and 641 NCCP).
- Selling of the property through judicial proceedings which ends in a public auction (Articles 636–675 NCCP). Following Law 42/2015, the auction will always be electronic. For this purpose, the Justice Administration has opened a web page called *'portal de subastas'*.
- The creditor can opt for keeping the property as owner following the conditions stated by law (Articles 650, 670–671 NCCP).
- Finally, the creditor can ask the judge to let him keep the property for management. In that case, he does not own the property, but he keeps the fruits and rents that the property produces to pay his credit. When the credit is paid, the property returns to its owner.

III. Enforcement of Other Types of Judgments

204. In these cases, where the creditor introduces his executive claim, the judge will notify the debtor that he has a period of time to comply with the judgment (Article 699 NCCP).

205. If the debtor has to render moveable property and he does not comply with the judgment, the judge, with the help of the police to enter premises, will give the property to the creditor. If the property is in an unknown place, the judge will ask the debtor of the whereabouts and if he does not answer he shall be held in contempt of court. If the property is never found, a sum of money, equivalent to the value of the property, will be given to the creditor (Article 701 NCCP).

206. If the debtor has to render immovable property, the judge will order whatever is necessary to transfer the property and to record the deed in a public registry. If the property is the house of the debtor, he has one month to vacate the premises, otherwise he shall be evicted. If the property is the house of a third person, he shall be notified of the transfer of property and he has ten days to present a legal title to occupy the premises. If he does not have a valid title, an order of eviction will be issued (Articles 703–704 NCCP).

207. When the judgment orders the debtor to do something, the court will give him or her a ten-day term to comply (Article 705 NCCP).

If the debtor does not comply, the NCCP distinguishes two cases:

(1) Those cases where the personal characteristics of the debtor were not taken into account in the obligation. If in this case the debtor does not comply, the creditor can choose, between the following options: A third person will carry out the obligation or he can ask for a monetary compensation (Article 706 NCCP).
(2) Those cases where the personal characteristics of the debtor were taken into account in the obligation. In this second case, the debtor must expose to the court why he does not want to comply with the judgment. The creditor can choose between a monetary compensation or he can ask the judge to fine the debtor on a monthly basis until he complies with his obligations (Article 709 NCCP).

208. When the debtor has been ordered in the judgment to do nothing and he does not comply, he shall be ordered to undo whatever he has done. If it is not possible to undo what has been done, a monetary compensation will be given to the creditor (Article 710 NCCP).

§2. Recognition and Enforcement of Foreign Judgments

I. Rules Applicable in the Absence of a Treaty

209. Foreign judgments do not have legal force in Spain unless an *exequatur* was granted. The action for 'exequatur' has two functions: First, it has a declaratory function and when the exequatur is granted, the foreign judgment is equivalent to a Spanish one. Second, the foreign judgment which has been recognized is enforceable. Usually, recognition is sought because a party wants to enforce the judgment, but it is possible that the party wants the recognition for other purposes, especially res judicata.

210. In this matter, Articles 951-958 LEC 1881 were in force until July 2015 when Law 29/2015 was approved (International legal Cooperation in civil and commercial matters). In accordance with Article 2 of Law 29/2015, International Legal Cooperation is governed by: (a) the rules of the European Union and international treaties signed by Spain; (b) special rules of domestic Law; and (c) finally as provided by LCJI.

211. Reciprocity has disappeared as an applicable source since Article 3.2 states that it is not enforceable. However, the Government may establish that Spanish authorities will not cooperate with the authorities of a foreign state when there is a repeated denial of cooperation or a legal prohibition to provide it by the authorities of that State.

212. Article 46 of Law 29/2015 establishes the reasons why a foreign resolution will not be recognized:

– When contrary to public order.

- When the resolution has been dictated with manifest infraction against the rights of defence of either party.
- When the foreign resolution was pronounced on a matter in which the Spanish courts are exclusively competent or, with regards to other matters, if the jurisdiction of the judge or origin is unreasonable. Competence is presumed reasonable when it is based on criteria similar to those provided in Spanish law.
- When the judgment is irreconcilable (contradictory) with resolutions dictated in Spain.
- When the resolution is irreconcilable (contradictory) with another ruling dictated previously in another State when this prior resolution meets the necessary conditions for recognition in Spain.
- When there is pending litigation in Spain between the same parties and with the same action initiated prior to the foreign process.

213. Unless stated otherwise by treaties, the competent court to recognize foreign judgments are the courts of first instance or the Commercial Courts (according to matter) of the domicile or place of residence of the party against which the exequatur was requested or of the people affected by the sentences and finally the competent judge shall be from the venue where the sentence has to be executed or where the sentences produce their effects. Finally, the competent judge shall be from where the claim of exequatur is filed (Article 52 LCJI).

The proceedings begin upon filing of a claim, as established in Article 54 LCJI in relation to Article 399 NCCP. It will be the plaintiff who requests the recognition and the defendant will be the party against whom the recognition or enforcement is sought. In the same claim, recognition and enforcement can be requested, but enforcement will not proceed until the judgment has been recognized.

The claim must be introduced with the following documents: a) Original or authenticated copy of the foreign resolution, duly legalized or apostilled; b) if the judgment was rendered by default, the document which proves that the defendant was duly notified of the existing proceedings; c) any document which proves the foreign resolution is final and enforceable; and d) the required translations in accordance with Article 144 NCCP.

The defendant should be notified of the claim and he/she has thirty days to file an opposition against it.

Finally, the judge will decide by decree (Article 54 LCJI). This resolution can be appealed. Against the resolution of the Provincial Court cassation or an extraordinary appeal for procedural infringement may be lodged in accordance with the general norms of the NCCP (Article 55 LCJI).

The Public Attorney will always intervene in this procedure (Article 54.8 LCJI) and the parties must be represented and defended according to the general rules of the NCCP. Free legal assistance can be provided according with the provisions of Law 1/1996 (Article 53 LCJI).

II. International Treaties

214. Spain has ratified several treaties for the enforcement of foreign judgments. They are bilateral and multilateral. Spain has signed treaties with the following countries: Switzerland (1896), Colombia (1908), France (1969), Italy (1973), Germany (1983), Austria (1984), Czech and Slovak Republic (1987), Uruguay (1987), Israel (1989), Mexico (1989), Brazil (1989), Russia (1990) China (1992), Bulgaria (1993), Morocco (1997) and Rumania (1997), El Salvador (2000), Tunisia (2001), Algeria (2005), Mauritania (2006).

215. Of the multilateral treaties, the most important was the Convention of Brussels of 28 September 1968, which Spain signed after becoming a Member State of the European Community in 1986. Council Regulation (EC) 44/2001 of 22 December 2000 substitutes the Convention of Brussels and Regulation EU 1215/2012, of December 12, is now in force (since 10 January 2015). Regulation 1215/2012 sets the principle that 'a judgement given in a Member State shall be recognized in other Member States without any special procedure being required' (Article 36). Nevertheless, Regulation 1215/2012 states a few restrictions to this principle, especially when the judgment is contrary to public policy; when the judgment was given in default of appearance (if the defendant was not served with the document which instituted the proceedings or with an equivalent document in sufficient time and in such a way to enable him or her to arrange for his defence, unless the defendant failed to commence proceedings to challenge the judgment when it was possible to do so); if the judgment is irreconcilable with a judgment given between the same parties in the Member State addressed; if the judgment is irreconcilable with an earlier judgment given in another Member State or in a third State involving the same cause of action and between the same parties, provided that the earlier judgments fulfil the conditions necessary for its recognition in the Member State addressed or if the judgment conflicts with sections 3, 4 or 5 of Chapter II (where the policyholder, the insured, a beneficiary of the insurance contract, the injured party or the employee was the defendant) or section 6 of Chapter II (Article 45).

In as similar way, Article 39 sets the principle that a 'judgement given in a Member State which is enforceable in that Member State shall be enforceable in the other Member State without any declaration of enforceability being required'. On the application of the person against whom enforcement is sought, the enforcement of a judgment shall be refused where one of the grounds referred to in Article 4 is found to exist (Article 46).

Under no circumstances may a foreign judgment given in a Member State be reviewed as to its substance in the Member State addressed (Article 52).

216. Any interested party may, in accordance with the procedure provided for in subsection 2 of section 1 of Chapter III, apply for a decision that there are no grounds for refusal of recognition (Article 36.2).

On the application of the person against whom enforcement is sought, the enforcement of a judgment shall be refused where one of the grounds referred in Article 45 is found to exist (Article 46). The procedure for refusal of enforcements shall, in so far as it is not covered by Regulation 1215/2012, be governed by the law of the Member State addressed (Article 47.2)

The Court shall decide on the application for refusal of enforcement without delay (Article 48). The decision on the application for refusal of enforcement may be appealed against by either party (Article 49).

The Convention of Lugano (1988) is similar to the Convention of Brussels and includes the countries of the European Association of Free Trade.

Chapter 2. Protective Measures

217. Book III, Title VI of the NCCP, is dedicated to establish the rules of protective measures. It is completely different from the old regulation of LEC 1881.

Protective measures can be requested to be sure that the future judgment shall be effective and enforceable.

Protective measures have the following characteristics under Spanish law (Article 726 NCCP):

- They do not have a purpose in themselves because they are instrumental in relation with the judgment that shall be issued.
- Protective measures are provisional and they only last for a limited period of time.
- Protective measures can be changed during the proceedings.
- According to Article 728 NCCP, in order to authorize a protective measure it is necessary the debt appears to be well founded (*fumus boni iuris*). Generally, this requisite is fulfilled with documents but another type of evidence is allowed.
- There is possibility of danger in recovering a debt if a protective measure is not taken (periculum in mora).

218. These measures can be requested with the claim or even prior, in case of urgency. In this latter case, the claim has to be introduced within twenty days after the authorization of the measures (Article 730 NCCP).

219. There is a list of measures in Article 727 NCCP, but this list is not exhaustive. Some elements mentioned seizure for security, attachment or real property, administration of property, escrow, deposits, preventive inscription in public records, court orders to cease an activity, suspension of decisions of the organs of a legal person, etc.

220. Generally, the proceedings to authorize protective measures are adversarial. Exceptionally, for example in case of emergency, the court can adopt them without hearing the defendant. Articles 733 and 734 of the NCCP establish that both parties shall be summoned to a hearing to take protective measures and after the hearing the judge will decide if protective measures are allowed or not. The decision can be appealed (Article 736 NCCP).

When the protective measure has been adopted without hearing the defendant, he can oppose it within twenty days (Article 739 NCCP) and the case will be decided in a hearing (Article 741 NCCP).

221. The defendant can ask the judge to substitute the protective measures taken by a bond (Article 747 NCCP). This decision is taken after a hearing and cannot be appealed (Article 747 NCCP).

Part X. Arbitration

§1. Introduction

222. Arbitration is a method of resolving disputes not by a State judge but by a private judge that the parties can choose by themselves. The origin of arbitration is a contract. The agreement of the parties is generally a clause of a contract, but can be an independent one.

223. Law of 23 December 2003 establishes the rules governing arbitration. According to Article 2 of the law, arbitration is possible to solve disputes in matters of free disposition and Article 1 excludes matters subject to labour Courts.

224. There are two types of arbitration according to Article 34 of LA:

(1) Arbitration in law. In this case, arbitrators decide the case according to the sources of law.
(2) Arbitration in equity. Arbitrators are not subject to the law and they can decide according to their common sense.

If the parties do not state clearly that the arbitration is in law, then arbitration in equity is presumed.

225. The arbitration contract must express unequivocally the will of the parties to submit existing or future disputes to the jurisdiction of an arbitration court, stating the obligation of the parties of complying with the arbitration award. (Article 9 LA)

The contract has to be in writing. It is valid although it is not written in a single document. The contract can be presumed of an exchange of letters or other ways of communication including optical or electronic media (Article 9.3).

226. In the arbitration contract or in a latter moment, the parties can appoint the arbitrators and they can determine the rules of the proceedings (Articles 15 and 25 LA).

The parties can choose a specialized legal person to carry out the arbitration (Article 14 LA).

§2. Arbitrators and Arbitral Tribunal

227. The arbitrator must be a person with legal capacity. If the arbitration is in law, he or she must be a person with a law degree unless expressly agreed against (Article 15 LA).

The arbitrators must be appointed in an odd number. If the parties do not agree on the number of arbitrators, then the number must be one (Article 12 LA). If a legal person is managing the arbitration, arbitrators will be appointed according to the rules of proceedings set by the legal person (Article 14.2 LA).

Arbitrators have to accept their appointment (Article 16 LA) and they must fulfil their duties. In other case, they will be liable (Article 16 LA).

They must be paid and they can ask the parties for money to cover the expenses that the arbitration can cause (Article 21 LA).

If the parties do not agree on the appointment of the arbitrators, the rules laid down in Article 15 LA shall apply, with the possibility of intervention by the State Court.

§3. Conduct of Arbitral Proceedings

228. According to Article 24 LA, arbitration proceedings are adversarial and the rights to be heard and equality before the arbitration court have to be respected. Proceeding rules can be set by the parties or by the rules of proceedings of the legal person managing the arbitration. Lawyer or representatives are not required, but the parties can appoint a lawyer to represent them. The parties will generally decide the place of the proceedings and also the language (Article 26 and 28 LA).

Arbitrators are not bound by strict rules of procedure or by special terms, but they must give a period of time to the parties to make the initial pleadings (Article 29 LA). Unless agreed to the contrary, arbitrators, ex officio or requested by the parties, can name one or more expert witnesses (Article 32 LA)

First instance judges can help the arbitrators in this matter by their request (Article 33 LA). The adversarial principle rules in all evidence proceedings.

§4. Arbitral Award

229. As we said above, the arbitrators can decide in accord with the law or in equity. Except otherwise stated by the parties, the arbitrators have a six-month term to render the award. This period of time can be extended by mutual agreement of the parties before its end. If the award is not issued before the end of the term, the arbitration proceedings will end and the arbitrators will be ceased, but the arbitration agreement is valid (Article 37 LA).

230. The award has to be in writing and Article 37 LA establishes that it must be substantiated.

The award shall be approved by a majority vote. In case of a draw, the President opinion shall prevail (Article 35).

231. In the award the arbitrators will establish who has to pay the cost of arbitration (Article 37 LA).

232. An arbitration award discharges the arbitrators, but the parties can ask the arbitrators to correct any material error or they can ask the arbitrators to interpret the award or complete it (Article 39 LA).

233. The arbitration award is res judicata (Article 43 LA) and can be enforced as a judgment. Enforcement may be suspended when an appeal has been filed (Article 45 LA). The enforcement will be in accordance with the NCCP, by the first instance judge of the place where the award was issued.

§5. Recourse against Arbitral Award

234. The arbitration award can be reviewed by the Provincial Court in whose province the award was granted. This type of review is called 'recurso de anulación' and it is possible only for the motives stated in Article 41 LA:

(a) Nullity of the arbitration contract.
(b) Infringement of the norms to appoint the arbitrators or infringement of essential norms of the arbitration proceedings stated by law or the agreement by the parties.
(c) The arbitrators have decided questions that cannot be subject to arbitration or they have decided questions that are not part of the arbitration agreement.
(d) The award is contrary to public policy.
(e) When appointing the arbitrators or in the arbitration process, the agreement has not been fulfilled by the parties or the parties or the law has not been followed.

The claim has to be filed within two months after the notification of the award (Article 42 NCCP). Oral proceedings will be used. The ruling cannot be appealed (Article 42 LA).

§6. Recognition and Enforcement of International or Foreign Awards

235. Article 46 LA states that a foreign award shall be enforced in Spain according to the Convention of New York of 1958. It is important to underline that bilateral treaties on judgments can be applied to arbitration. Article 46 LA reads that a foreign award is an award that is not granted in Spain.

The proceedings to be followed are those foreseen in the law for judgments rendered by foreign courts.

Part XI. Mediation

Chapter 1. Legislation/Definitions

236. Law 5/2012 of July 6 regulates mediation in civil and commercial matters. This Act incorporates Directive 52/2008, of the European Parliament and the Council.

Mediation is based on free will of the parties and the intervention of a mediator. The mediator must intervene actively in order to facilitate conflict resolution between the parties. The mediator helps to find a dialogued resolution which is voluntarily accepted by the parties.

Chapter 2. Rights that can be Subject to Mediation

237. The Mediation Law applies to mediation in civil and commercial matters as long as it affects rights and obligations that the parties may freely dispose of (Article 2.1 Mediation Law). This article has been modified by Law 7/2017 of November 2 to include mediation in relation to the rights of consumers.

It expressly excludes:

- criminal mediation;
- mediation in administrative matters;
- labour mediation.

Chapter 3. Mediation Agreement

238. Mediation is voluntary. There must be a written agreement in which the parties are willing to submit to mediation their existing or potential future disputes. The agreement compels them to attempt the mediation process. No one is obligated to remain in the mediation process or to reach an agreement (Article 6 Mediation Law).

Chapter 4. Persons/Institutions that can Act as Mediator

239. A mediator may be a natural person or a legal entity. Legal entities must appoint a natural person (Article 11.1 Mediation Law).

Mediators must have liability insurance due to exposure to legal actions stemming from the mediation conduct (Article 11.3 Mediation Law).

Mediators must be impartial. The parties must be informed of any circumstances which could affect their impartiality such as:

- Personal, contractual or a business relationship with one of the parties;
- Direct or indirect interest in the outcome of the mediation;
- If, under any circumstance, the mediator has acted in favour of one or several of the parties, with the exception of mediation. In these cases, mediation may continue if the parties expressly consent to do so (Article 13 Mediation Law).

240. A mediator must facilitate communication between the parties and ensure that all required information and advice are provided and he or she must actively encourage the parties to reach an agreement in compliance with the law. Finally, the mediator must provide a statement to the parties if they decide not to continue mediation proceedings (Article 13 Mediation Law).

241. Mediators are responsible for any damage they may cause. The party has direct action against the mediators and against the mediation institution.

242. Mediation institutions are public or private entities, Spanish or foreign, and corporations under public law that have, among their purpose, the promotion of mediation. They should facilitate the access and administration of mediation, including the appointment of mediators. They must guarantee transparency in that appointment.

Mediation institutions will publicly list the mediation providers who act within their scope. They will at least inform of their professional training, specialty and experience in the field of mediation in which they work (Article 5.1 Mediation Law).

Mediation institutions may implement mediation systems via electronic means, especially for disputes which involve monetary claims (Article 5.2 Mediation Law).

Chapter 5. Mediation Procedure

243. Mediation proceedings can be initiated when there is a mediation agreement between the parties or when parties agree to mediation. A party must present a request for mediation. If a judicial proceeding has already started, the parties may request a suspension of such proceedings (Article 16 Mediation Law).

244. The mediator will summon the parties for an information session. A non-justified absence of the party will be considered a waiver of mediation (Article 17.1 Mediation Law).

The mediator will inform the parties of:

- possible reasons which may affect his/her impartiality;
- his/her profession, education and experience;
- characteristics of the mediation, cost and organization of the procedure;
- deadline to begin the mediation proceedings;
- effects of the agreement which may be reached (Article 17.1 Mediation Law).

245. The mediation procedure begins with a session in which the parties express their will to resolve their dispute through mediation.

The following shall be recorded:

- Identification of the parties.
- The appointment of the mediator and, when appropriate, the name of the mediation institution or the acceptance of the mediator appointed.
- Matter of dispute.
- The course of action and the maximum duration foreseen of the mediation proceedings.
- Information of the cost of mediation.
- A statement by the parties indicating voluntary acceptance of mediation and that they assume the obligations derived from it.
- Venue and language of the proceedings (Article 19.1 Mediation Law).

The session must be documented in writing. It will also be noted if mediation has been attempted without effect (Article 19.2 Mediation Law).

246. Mediation will be as brief as possible and the number of sessions should be kept to as few as possible (Articles 20 Mediation Law).

247. The mediator shall convene the parties ahead of time for each session. Likewise, he/she shall conduct the sessions and facilitate an equal and balanced communication of the points in dispute between the parties.

248. The communication of the mediator and the parties may or may not be simultaneous.

The mediator has to separately communicate to each party when the sessions will take place, without detriment to the confidentiality of what has been addressed. The mediator cannot communicate or distribute the information or documents that the party has provided except if expressly authorized (Article 21 Mediation Law).

The parties in dispute must have an equal opportunity to participate in the mediation proceedings (Article 7 Mediation Law).

The parties may freely organize the mediation process (Article 10.1 Mediation Law).

The parties will act according to the principles of loyalty, good faith and mutual respect. The parties may not initiate judicial or extrajudicial actions while the mediation process is ongoing with respect to the same cause of action. Nonetheless, they could request precautionary or urgent measures to prevent irreversible loss of property or rights (Article 10.2 Mediation Law). If one of the parties initiates a judicial process, and a mediation agreement already exists, the other party may file a motion to contest jurisdictions (Article 10.2 Mediation Law).

The parties should cooperate with the mediator (Article 10.3 Mediation Law).

249. The mediator must maintain the balance between the parties' positions and respect the view they express, without the mediator being able to act to the detriment or interest of any of them (Article 7.1 Mediation Law).

250. The proceedings should take place so that the parties are able to freely reach an agreement on their own.

251. The mediation proceedings and the corresponding documents are confidential. The confidentiality principle extends to the mediator (who is protected by professional secrecy), the mediation institutions and the parties who intervene. The information obtained from the proceedings cannot be revealed (Articles 9.1 Mediation Act).

The mediators and the parties who participate in mediation proceedings cannot be forced to declare or provide documents in judicial proceedings or arbitration except: a) when expressly authorized in writing by the parties or b) when the information is requested by the judge in a criminal case (Article 9.2 Mediation Law). The infraction of the duty of confidentiality gives rise to liability (Article 9.3 Mediation Law).

Chapter 6. Settlement Agreement

252. Mediation may end with or without an agreement.

The end of proceedings without an agreement may be due to the following reasons:

- All or one of the parties decides to end the proceedings by informing the mediator.
- The maximum period agreed for the duration of mediation has elapsed.
- There are irreconcilable differences between the parties or another cause which may determine its conclusion. These circumstances should be taken into consideration by the mediator.
- If the mediator renounces to continue mediation or the parties reject the mediator, the mediation proceedings will only end if a new mediator cannot be appointed (Article 22 Mediation Law).

253. If an agreement is reached, it will be recorded in a document in a clear and comprehensive manner. The mediator and parties will sign the minutes and a copy will be given to each one of the parties. It will be noted if any one of the parties does not want to sign (Article 22.3 Mediation Law).

254. An agreement may be reached on all or part of the disputes subject to mediation.

The agreement should include:

- Identity of the parties.
- The address of each party.
- Place and date.
- Obligations each party agrees to.
- Identity of the mediator.
- Compliance with all procedural requirements.

255. The mediator shall inform the parties of the binding nature of the agreement reached and that they may request that it be recorded in a public deed to set up their agreement as an enforceable document (Article 23 Mediation Law).

256. The law allows for some or all of the proceedings to take place via electronic means, video conference or similar means. The identity of the parties must be guaranteed and mediation principles established by law must be respected.

These means will preferably be used for mediation if the quantity of the dispute is less than EUR 600 (Article 24 Mediation Law).

257. The mediation agreement may be recorded in a public deed. The notary must verify that all legal requirements have been met and the content is not contrary to law. If an agreement is reached during mediation initiated after the beginning of a judicial proceeding, it may be validated in accordance with the NCCP

(Article 25 Mediation Law). In this case, the competent court to enforce the agreement is the court that validated it (Article 26 Mediation Law). In all other cases, the competent court to enforce the agreement will be the Court of First Instance of the place where the agreement was reached in accordance with Article 545.2 NCCP.

258. The parties must pay the cost of mediation proceedings on an equal basis except when otherwise agreed to by the parties. The mediator may request an advance of the cost of the mediation. If the parties do not pay the sum of money requested by the mediator, the mediator may end the mediation proceedings (Article 15 Mediation Law).

Chapter 7. Setting Aside a Settlement Agreement

259. Nullity of the settlement agreement may be pursued if there is one of the causes for invalidity of a contract according to the CC (Article 23.4 Mediation Law). The party that sustains the nullity of the agreement must initiate judicial proceedings before the competent court in order to obtain a judgment of nullity. General rules of the NCCP apply in the proceedings.

Chapter 8. International Mediation

260. A mediation agreement may be recognized and enforced in Spain according to the rules of the European Union, the international treaties which Spain is part of and the International Cooperation in Civil and Commercial Matters Law.

The mediation agreement must be recorded in a public deed in order to be enforceable unless a foreign authority has already made a declaration of enforceability.

It is not possible to enforce a foreign deed which is contrary to Spanish public order (Article 27 Mediation Law).

Selected Bibliography

Aragoneses Martínez, S. *Los procesos declarativos ordinarios*. Madrid: La Ley, 2000.

Armenta Deu, T. *La ejecución provisional*. Madrid: La Ley, 2000.

Armenta Deu, T. *Lecciones de Derecho Procesal Civil*. 9th edn Madrid: Marcial Pons, 2016.

Bonet Navarro, A. *Los recursos en el proceso civil*. Madrid: La Ley, 2000.

Bonet Navarro, J. *El proceso cambiario*. Madrid: La Ley, 2000.

Bonet Navarro, J. *La prueba en el proceso civil: cuestiones fundamentales*, Madrid, 2009.

Castillo Felipe, R. *La oposición a la ejecución por defectos procesales: estudio del art. 559 LEC*. Pamplina:Thomson-Aranzadi, 2017.

Cordón, F. *Introducción al Derecho Procesal*. 3rd edn. Pamplona: actualizada, Eunsa, 1998.

Cordón Moreno, F. (eds) et al. *Comentarios a la Ley de Enjuiciamiento Civil*. Ed. Aranzadi, Pamplona, 2001.

Cordón Moreno, F., et al. *Comentarios a la Ley de Enjuciamiento Civil*. Ed. Aranzadi, Pamplona, 2001.

Cortés Domínguez, V. & V. Moreno Catena. *Introducción al Derecho Procesal*. 8th edn Valencia: Tirant lo Blanch, 2015.

Cortés Domínguez, V. & V. Moreno Catena. *Derecho Procesal Civil. Parte General*. 8th edn Valencia: Tirant lo Blanch, 2015.

Cortés Domínguez, V. & V. Moreno Catena. *Derecho Procesal Civil. Parte Especial*. 8th edn Valencia: Tirant lo Blanch, 2016.

De la Oliva Santos, A. & I. Díez-picazo Giménez. *El proceso de declaración*. 3rd edn. Ed. Centro de Estudios Ramón Areces, Madrid, 2004.

De la Oliva Santos, A., et al. *Comentarios a la Ley de Enjuiciamiento Civil*. Ed. Civitas, Madrid, 2001.

De la Oliva Santos, A., I. Díez Picazo Giménez & J. VegasTorres. *Introducción al Derecho Procesal*. 3rd edn Madrid: Centro de Estudios Ramón Areces, 2008.

De la Oliva Santos, A. & I. Díez Picazo Gimenez. *Ejecución forzosa y procesos especiales*. 3 edn Madrid: Centro de Estudios Ramóna Areces, 2005.

De la Oliva Santos, A., et al. *Comentarios a la Ley de Enjuiciamiento Civil*. Ed. Civitas, Madrid, 2001.

Fernández-Ballesteros, M.A., J.M. Rifá Soler & J.F. Valls Gombau (eds), *Comentarios a la Ley de Enjuiciamiento Civil*. Barcelona: Iurgium Editores, 2000.

Selected Bibliography

Font Serra, E. *El dictamen de peritos y el reconocimiento judicial en el proceso civil.* Madrid: La Ley, 2000.
García Inchausti, F. *La acumulación de acciones en el proceso civil.* Madrid: La Ley, 2000.
Garciandía González, P. *La tasación de costas en el proceso civil español: Ley 1/2000, de 7 de enero, de Enjuiciamiento Civil.* Pamplona: Aranzadi, 2001.
García-Rostán Calvín, G, *El recurso de apelación en el proceso civil.*Madrid: Colex, 2001.
Gimeno Sendra, V. *Introducción al Derecho Procesal.* 3rd edn Madrid: Colex, 2015.
Gimeno Sendra, V. *Derecho Procesal Civil.* 6th edn Madrid: Colex, 2010.
Herrero Perezagua. *La representación y defensa de las partes y las costas en el proceso civil.* Madrid: La Ley, 2000.
Jiménez Conde, F., et al. *Manual de Derecho Procesal Civil, 2nd edn,* Murcia, DM, 2015.
Montero Aroca, J., et al. *El nuevo proceso civil.* Valencia: Tirant lo Blanch, 2000.
Montero Aroca, J., et al. *Derecho Jurisdiccional I. Parte General.* 24th edn Valencia: Tirant lo Blanch, 2016.
Montero Aroca, J., et al. *Derecho Jurisdiccional II. Proceso Civil.* 24th edn Valencia: Tirant lo Blanch, 2016.
Montes Reyes, A. *División judicial de patrimonios.* Madrid: La Ley, 2000.
Moreno Catena, V. & V. Cortés Domínguez (Coord,). *La nueva Ley de Enjuiciamiento Civil.* Madrid: Tecnos, 2000.
Nieva Fenoll, Jordi, *Derecho Procesal I. Introducción.* Marcial Pons. Madrid, 2014.
Ormazábal Sánchez, G. *La prueba documental y los medios e instrumentos idóneos para reproducir imágenes, sonidos o archivos y conocer datos.* Madrid: La Ley, 2000.
Ormazábal Sánchez, G. *Introducción al Derecho Procesal.* 6th edn Madrid: Marcial Pons, 2016.
Ortells Ramos, M., et al. *Derecho Procesal Civil.* 16th edn Pamplona: Aranzadi, 2016.
Ortells Ramos, M., et al. *Introducción al Derecho Procesal.* 6th edn Valencia, 2016.
Ortells Ramos, M. *Las medidas cautelares.* Madrid: La Ley, 2000.
Ramos Méndez, F. *El sistema procesal Español.* Bosch, Barcelona, 2000.
Ramos Méndez, F. *Jurisprudencia procesal civil internacional.* Bosch, Barcelona, 2001.
Robles Garzón, J.A., et al. *Conceptos básicos de Derecho Procesal Civil.* 5th edn Madrid: Tecnos, 2013.
Ruiz Moreno, J.M. *El proceso especial de filiación, paternidad y maternidad.* Madrid: La Ley, 2000.
Samanes Ara, C. *Las partes en el proceso civil.* Madrid: La Ley, 2000.
Senés Motilla, C. *Disposiciones generales sobre la ejecución forzosa.* Madrid: La Ley, 2000.
Sigüenza López, J. *Sistema Judicial Español.* 6th edn, Murcia: Laborum, 2017.
Tapia Fernández. *El objeto del proceso: alegaciones, sentencia, cosa juzgada.* Madrid: La Ley, 2000.
Tomás Tomás, S. *La administración concursal. Claves para entender su actual régimen jurídico.* Navarra: Civitas Thomson Reuters, 2014.

Index

The numbers here refer to paragraph numbers.

Index

Made in the USA
Monee, IL
13 September 2026

62974286R00059